"*For thou didst form my inward parts;
Thou didst weave me in my
mother's womb. I will give thanks to Thee,
for I am fearfully and wonderfully made:
wonderful are thy works, and my soul
knows it very well.*"

— From Psalm 139

SANCTITY
of LIFE

CHARLES R. SWINDOLL

SANCTITY
of LIFE

THE
INESCAPABLE
ISSUE

FOREWORD BY
DR. JAMES C. DOBSON

WORD PUBLISHING
Dallas · London · Vancouver · Melbourne

SANCTITY OF LIFE

Unless otherwise indicated, Scripture quotations used in this
book are from the New American Standard Bible, © 1960,
1962, 1963, 1968, 1971, 1972, 1973, 1975, 1977 by The Lock-
man Foundation. Used by permission.

ISBN 0-8499-3242-4

01239 AGF 98765432

Printed in the United States of America

With great admiration, this volume is dedicated
to the young women who lived in our home
while carrying their babies.
Though unmarried, they refused an abortion.
Tearfully, each one released her infant
to the loving arms of adoptive parents,
whose long-awaited dreams were fulfilled.
My family and I thank God upon every remembrance
of their courage and unselfishness.

Contents

Foreword

I was working in my office at Focus On The Family recently when the telephone rang. A minute or two later, my secretary came in to inform me that Dr. Chuck Swindoll was on the line. He had called to tell me about this book on abortion, and to describe his great burden to speak out boldly against the killing of unborn babies. He said the Lord had been speaking to him, and he intended to respond with intensity in his church, in the print media, and on the radio.

As my good friend described his intensified sense of mission, I was fighting back the tears. I knew, of course, that Chuck is highly respected and loved in the Christian community. Because he has now addressed the issues head-on, there will be precious babies brought into the world who would otherwise have been killed. Many little boys and girls, each worth more than the possessions of the entire world, will someday owe their very lives to the influence Dr. Swindoll will have on their mothers and their families.

Though it may be difficult for some pro-life veterans to comprehend, making a strong public statement against abortion was an evolving decision in Chuck's mind. It is not a position at which he arrived with ease. He has not wanted to drag the church into the political arena, and I applaud that caution. There are great dangers in linking the cause of Christ to legislative issues, political parties or social movements of the day. Thus, many pastors have held back in the abortion issue. Their obligation, they felt, was to preach the Word, and from that Truth will come the moral application in society.

But on this issue of abortion, we are confronted with one of the most terrible evils of all times. The Nazis killed six million Jews and "undesirables" during World War II, but we in the United States—this great bastion of liberty and protection for the weak —have now slaughtered more than twenty million innocent babies! We have mercilessly torn them to pieces without anesthetic and poisoned them within their mothers' wombs. My God! Forgive us for this wickedness! We know from Scripture that the Lord is infinitely tender and compassionate toward the little children with whom He has blessed us. What must He be feeling now, as we spill their blood for our own convenience and economy? How can we as Christians continue to sit in our services and ignore this unprecedented crime against humanity? As Dr.

Swindoll writes in this book, "Remaining silent . . . is no longer an option."

To pastors and laymen alike who have not yet joined the pro-life crusade, I urge you to read carefully the words that follow. Let the Lord speak to you as you ask, with Chuck, "What would He have *me* do to protect the unborn child?" If you save only one little boy or girl in a lifetime, your effort will not have been in vain.

Thank you, my friend Chuck, for listening to the Holy Spirit and for responding to His urging. We are glad you are numbered among the rag-tag, wounded, outmanned and outgunned little army of pro-life warriors. We've lost about 80 consecutive battles now, but we fully intend to win the *last* one!

James C. Dobson, Ph.D.
Focus On The Family

Introduction:
From My Heart
to Yours

I am a pastor. I have been involved in ministry since early 1959, the year I was discharged from the Marine Corps and entered seminary. During these decades I have been directly in touch with the needs of people. Refusing to remain aloof from the pain and brokenness of humanity, my wife and I have seen firsthand the heartache brought on by wrong choices and irresponsible decisions. Rather than hardening us, these up-close-and-personal years in the real world have deepened our understanding, softened our spirits, and given us a compassion neither of us possessed in our earlier years. As our eyes have been opened, our hearts have been broken.

God has chosen to extend the boundaries of our ministry far beyond my expectations. As this has happened, I have been allowed to witness a broader scene than many in ministry. Such exposure has enlarged my perspective and forced me to face issues I could have otherwise missed altogether or conveniently chosen to ignore.

Of all the issues I have encountered through all the years I have been engaged in people-related involvements, none are more significant than the sanctity of life and sexual purity. The ground swell of concern surrounding each has made them the inescapable issues of our times. Remaining silent on either is no longer an option. I have spoken on both in recent months. The response was so overwhelming I felt compelled to put my thoughts into print.

The book you hold in your hand is the result of that decision. As you can see by its size, it is not meant to be an exhaustive treatment of the issues. Many other volumes, far more thorough than mine, deal with the subjects in much greater detail. My desire, however, is to address the essentials succinctly, biblically, and compassionately . . . leaving you room to reason your way through the mine field without getting blown away in confusion. It is my hope that you will feel informed rather than insulted, encouraged to think rather than forced to agree on every point, and ultimately motivated to make the best decisions based on the timeless principles of Scripture.

In the final analysis, the ball is in your court. You are the one who must decide, then respond on the basis of that decision. As a pastor, I appeal to your heart throughout this book. Open its door and let the truth in. If you do, you will be surprised at how quickly the fog will lift and how clearly the issues will appear. At that point, the right decisions will no longer seem confusing and complicated. They will, in fact, be incredibly simple.

Simple . . . but not easy.

Chuck Swindoll
Fullerton, California

SANCTITY
of LIFE

1

The Sanctity of Life

Not since the controversial issue of slavery ripped America apart at the seams has one subject troubled our country like abortion. It is virtually impossible to pick up a national periodical or, for that matter, a daily newspaper without seeing an article, a column, a story, or an editorial either directly or indirectly related to abortion. Physicians and politicians, educators and newscasters, radio and television talk-show hosts, feminists and lobbyists alike are never far from discussing the subject. The heat is rising and there is every reason to believe the intensity of the debate will only increase. Like slavery, abortion will neither solve its own dilemmas nor quietly go away. There is every reason to believe it will be the significant topic of debate throughout the decade of the 1990s. Not even the President of the United States can sustain a noncommittal stance.

In light of all this, an enormous amount of emotion swirls in the abortion arena. Shouting matches at abortion-clinic sit-ins are commonplace. It isn't unusual for some representing the pro-life position to spend time behind bars for blocking entrances to abortion clinics. Others, with even greater passion, have set clinics on fire. And those representing the proabortion position, with equal vigor, declare that women are free to choose . . . that such a choice is their right. Perhaps the statement most commonly expressed in the heat of the debate comes from those who declare, "I may not choose to have an abortion, but I'd never force my opinion on another," as they back away from the issue altogether, refusing any involvement in the debate. All the while, babies continue to be aborted by the thousands every day.

If the issue of slavery had been handled in that manner, to this day there would be shacks out back, the mistreatment of blacks, and a majority of Americans still looking the other way. It may be more comfortable to adopt a passive stance with regard to the abortion issue. It certainly would be the least offensive response. But who, with a clear conscience, can sit back, say little, and do nothing while babies continue to be killed? If the mistreated blacks needed strong-minded advocates in the mid-nineteenth century, how much more do unborn children need strong-minded advocates today. It has come to the time where the most dangerous place to be in America is not in the inner city where gangs threaten innocent lives or in angry prisons where only the fit survive . . . but in the womb of a mother who is being told if she doesn't really want the baby, an abortion is the solution. May I ask? How would you like to be that baby inside the womb of a woman who isn't sure she wants you to live any longer?

John Willke, president of the National Right to Life, asks the right questions:

> . . . Since when does anyone's right to live depend upon someone else wanting them? Killing the unwanted is a monstrous evil. . . .
>
> So, should a woman have the right to choose? I have a right to free speech, but not to shout "fire" in a theater. A person's right to anything stops when it injures or kills another living human. . . .
>
> The pivotal question is, should any civilized nation give to one citizen the absolute right to kill another to solve that first person's personal problem?[1]

My Purpose in Writing This Book

In light of these conflicting voices on the horizon and the undeniable reality that the issue isn't going away and will not automatically solve itself, why would I write on something this controversial, this thorny? Four answers come to mind:

1. To inform you of the facts.

Surprisingly, many still do not know the scoop. Though the subject is the hot topic and occupies space in all the media, I am convinced that most have not been sufficiently informed of the facts. Due to limited space, I am forced to stay lean on statistics and stories, but be assured what I do present, though limited, is accurate and it represents only a tip of the iceberg. Perhaps my brevity will help to bring to the surface those matters that are of critical importance. I'll restrain the rhetoric for the sake of plain facts.

2. To help you gain courage.

It is easy to be intimidated. The thought of stepping into an arena as volatile as this one is not pleasant; it takes courage. Women who are pregnant and find themselves in an unhappy and/or unhealthy situation will naturally be tempted to "solve" their dilemma by getting an abortion. As one young mother-to-be once told me: "After all it's legal, it's available, and it removes the responsibility of having to deal with all the hassles." My hope is to give such women the courage to say no to an abortion.

On the other hand, there are some who have gotten an abortion and cannot pull out of the depression or get beyond the guilt. If you are in that particular situation, you need the ability to go on, you need the assurance God offers anyone who has made a regrettable decision and cannot seem to recover. My hope is to provide a "courage transfusion," which will give you some needed light at the end of this dismal tunnel. My next chapter focuses attention on that very real need.

Furthermore, courage is needed in all our lives if we plan to do more than just sit back, shake our heads, and think about how tragic these things really are. Right thinking leads to tough decisions, which are followed by some kind of action. My hope is to increase your level of courage so that you will respond in ways that are both appropriate and effective.

Another area of needed courage—perhaps the most important of all—is the courage to be sexually pure. Since such a high standard of morality has been ignored or scoffed at so often in the past decade, the thought of embracing it seems out of the question. As one so-called authority recently put it, "It's so obsolete it's laughable." I disagree; you may, as well. But to model moral purity, one needs courage. Hopefully, the latter half of this book will help stimulate that into action.

3.   To motivate you to be involved.

As I mentioned earlier, action follows thinking and deciding. Certainly, we need to be people of prayer. No major change ever occurred unless and until God's people prayed. But there must be more than prayer if we hope to stem the tide of this national tragedy. And speaking of being involved, let me assure you that I do not advocate only one specific reaction. There are several options available to us, all of which are at our disposal. My hope is that you will be motivated to get personally involved . . . to spend a portion of your energy doing something about the issues, which will make you part of the answer rather than part of the problem. In matters as intense as this one, passivity is an enemy.

Years before abortion had gained the public attention it now receives, my wife Cynthia and I were more than a little concerned about the plight facing unwed mothers. Over a period of several years, we opened our home to some of these young women. Each one lived among our family (four small children!), ate at our dining table, had a room she could call her own, and was given all the privileges our own children enjoyed: love, privacy, dignity, encouragement, and time to talk things through. Each woman carried her baby to full term and shortly thereafter released the infant to adoptive parents. Cynthia and I were there through it all—the loneliness, the discussions, the tears, the disillusionment, the reluctance, and yes, the courage. We shall never be the same, nor will our now-grown children who learned so much along with us. How grateful we are that we didn't stop with prayer. It was our *involvement* that made the difference.

At the end of this chapter I will mention many of the options from which you may choose. It is extremely important that you (1) select one with which you are comfortable and (2) refrain from judging another person for not choosing the option *you* prefer. Great grace is needed here. I know whereof I speak! It hurt when I was told over the phone recently that because I chose not to participate in a certain way as the caller told me I should, he responded angrily by assuring me I would "answer for it in the day of judgment." Such an exclusive, judgmental attitude polarizes an otherwise united front that various meaningful involvements provide. People need to be given the freedom to respond as God leads them.

4.   To declare a biblical basis for issues at hand.

Much has already been written on sanctity and morality. Most of those things in print are splendid, reliable, and sincere attempts at explaining what is happening and why. The logic and the conclusions make good sense. What concerns me, however, is not what is stated but what is left unsaid. There is technical data from the medical world and the legal profession, psychological insights, political policies, even practical advice. But almost without exception, there is an absence of biblical foundation and theological justification of what is being set forth. Hopefully, these pages will help you realize that the Bible is neither silent nor irrelevant when it comes to the sanctity of life and the importance of sexual purity. Without being "preachy," I want to communicate how clearly God has already spoken on the things that are of utmost concern.

For sure, He has warned us that days such as these would come:

> But realize this, that in the last days difficult times will come. For men will be lovers of self, lovers of money, boastful, arrogant, revilers, disobedient to parents, ungrateful, unholy, unloving, irreconcilable, malicious gossips, without self-control, brutal, haters of good, treacherous, reckless, conceited, lovers of pleasure rather than lovers of God (2 Tim. 3:1–4).

The "difficult times" predicted in Scripture is not a pretty picture. By the way, that word "difficult" is eloquent. The original Greek term could be rendered "painful, tragic, grievous." In another section of the New Testament, it is the descriptive term used to portray two men who were demonized, and it is there rendered "exceedingly violent" (Matt. 8:28). Such are the savage times in which we live.

Another equally vivid statement appears in the first-century letter to the Romans. We are told that people in these days will be characterized as being "without understanding, untrustworthy, unloving, unmerciful" (Rom. 1:31). How true! Putting it another way:

- Without understanding ...... senseless
- Untrustworthy .... faithless
- Unloving .... heartless
- Unmerciful .... ruthless

Having been in ministry for these many years, I am still amazed at the relevance of a Book as ancient as the Bible. A quick glance at those four synonyms is all it takes to see that they describe the thinking of a generation that is so self-absorbed, the mother's rights have eclipsed all other rights, even the right of that independent life within her which neither she nor her sexual partner created; God did. My passion is for folks to know how clearly Scripture speaks to these matters and then to encourage them to apply the truth God has revealed.

Abortion: No Longer a Private Decision

There was once a time when the decision to have an abortion was so private, so secretive, nobody dared mention it in public. Not only was it illegal, it was considered the most intimate of subjects. It was not uncommon for family members to know nothing (which is still true) and for the medical profession to view it with disdain. The whole thing was a private decision and those who did know usually looked the other way. No longer. It is now big business, impacting three major professions of our world: the political, the legal, and for sure the medical.

Several years ago one hundred professors of obstetrics signed a statement that declared abortion no longer a professional risk but a "medical responsibility."

It would be necessary for physicians to realize that abortion has become a predominantly social as

well as medical responsibility. For the first time, except for cosmetic surgery, doctors will be expected
to do an operation simply because the patient asks
that it be done. Granted, this changes the physician's traditional role, but it will be necessary to
make this change if we are to serve the new society
in which we live.[2]

I agree with the man who added this comment:

Abortion is no more purely a medical problem
just because the physician wields the curette than
chemical warfare is purely a problem for pilots because they press the lever releasing the chemical.[3]

Some physicians may be willing to perform
abortions, but many are not. In fact, an article based
on the *New York Times* News Service appeared in a
Los Angeles newspaper entitled, "'Fewer Doctors
Performing Abortions." It included a series of facts
regarding the unpopularity of the physician who declares herself or himself as a doctor who will perform abortions. In the article are statements that
reveal the trauma some physicians experience who
have been involved in doing abortions. It certainly
gives another side of the story not presented by proabortion activists.

Many obstetricians and gynecologists acknowledge that they feel great conflict about abortion.
A doctor who is an administrator at the National Institutes of Health—and is forbidden to

speak for attribution about the time when she performed abortions—said she used to carry them out because she felt strongly that abortions should be available.

But, she said, she had to prepare herself emotionally each time, and she often had a sleepless night before a scheduled abortion.

"It's a very tough thing for a gynecologist to do," she said. The emotions it arouses are so strong, she said, that doctors "don't talk to each other about it."

The doctor said she was performing an abortion on a 30-year-old doctor after she herself had just had a miscarriage.

She had been trying for seven years to become pregnant.

After the abortion, she said, "I just collapsed on the floor," overcome by her emotions.[4]

Some Significant Statistics

But wait. Just how widespread is the practice of abortion? Are we making much ado about nothing, or do we have a full-scale issue deserving of our immediate attention? You decide. Only the senseless, faithless, heartless, and ruthless could read the following statistical facts and remain unmoved.

To begin with, let's understand that medical authorities determine a person to be "alive" if there is either a detectable heartbeat or brain-wave activity. With that in mind, it is eye-opening for some to realize that unborn children have detectable heartbeats at eighteen days (two and one-half weeks) after conception and detectable brain-wave activity forty days (a little over five and one-half weeks) after conception. What is so shocking is that essentially 100 percent of all abortions occur after the *seventh week* of pregnancy.

Why are children aborted? The Alan Guttmacher Institute (the research arm of Planned Parenthood) states:

- 1 percent are victims of incest or rape
- 1 percent had fetal abnormalities
- 4 percent had a doctor who said their health would worsen if they continued the pregnancy
- 50 percent said they didn't want to be a single parent or they had problems in current relationships
- 66 percent stated they could not afford a child
- 75 percent said the child would interfere with their lives.[5]

There are numerous related statistics I could include, but this is sufficient to help us come to one major conclusion: 95-plus percent of children killed by abortion are killed for reasons of convenience; not incest, not rape, not the physical condition of the unborn, and not the threatened health of the mother.

When are children aborted? Fifty percent of all abortions are performed at eight weeks; 25 percent at nine to ten weeks; 14 percent at eleven to twelve weeks; 5 percent at thirteen to fifteen weeks; 4

percent at sixteen to twenty weeks; and 2 percent after twenty weeks.

How many children are aborted? Worldwide, 55 million unborn children are killed every year. If you are like me, you can't get your arms around that large a number. To help us do so, let me break it into days, hours, and minutes. Around the world, every day 150,685 children are killed by abortion; every hour, 6,278; and every minute, 105. Those are the reported cases.

If you are an American citizen, no doubt your greatest interest is in your own nation, as is mine. Let me break the abortions down to a national statistic: 1,600,000 babies are aborted in these United States every year. Per day, that's 4,383; per hour, that's 183; per minute, there are 3. That's correct, in America alone 3 children are killed every minute.[6]

Because I am a military veteran, for years I have been especially interested in Americans who were killed in combat. The number of American war casualties is a gripping reality, for sure. But when compared to the number of unborn children who have been killed since abortion was legalized, the contrast is shocking.

The chart on the following page makes the point better than I could ever describe. Read it and weep. Admittedly, these figures on abortion are now obsolete (remember, 4,383 are killed *every day*), but they illustrate the awful truth many would like us to ignore.

AMERICAN WAR CASUALTIES[7]

Each cross-mark represents 25,000 people killed. The war casualties represent all American combat-related deaths.

REVOLUTIONARY WAR	25,324	†
CIVIL WAR	498,332	††††††††††††††††††††
WORLD WAR I	116,708	†††††
WORLD WAR II	407,316	††††††††††††††††
KOREAN WAR	54,246	††
VIETNAM WAR	58,655	†††
WAR ON THE UNBORN . . . since abortion was legalized in 1973	20,000,000	†††††††††††††††††††††††† ...

This is no minor skirmish that is happening. This is war. And the pathetic tragedy of it all is that those who are being killed can neither represent themselves before a court of law nor defend themselves from sure death. Lives are being taken brutally, tragically, and thoughtlessly. It has come to the place where, more often than not, abortion is little more than a convenient method of contraception.

Some Insightful Scriptures

I can hear a few passionate pro-life activists urging me to turn to the verse that says, "Thou shalt not get an abortion," so everyone will understand that the issue, so far as the Bible goes, is a slam-dunk. Only one problem with that request: There is no such verse. How simple it would be if all injustices were clearly addressed in objective verses of Scripture . . . but they are not. In fact, many of the evils and struggles of society are not that clearly defined in the Bible. Since that is true, we must search for principles in God's timeless Word that assist us in coming to correct conclusions. By thinking through the logic, or if I may, the syllogism of logic in the Scriptures, we are often able to arrive at positions that are virtually airtight.

Let's take a look at several scriptural statements that will give us an understanding of how God views these issues.

In the first chapter of the Bible, Genesis 1, we find some helpful, uncomplicated information that will give us insight into the issue.

The first chapter of Genesis is the account of God's creative actions as He originated all things. God has created matter. He has made the world and its surrounding universe. He has separated night from day, earth from sea, mountains from valleys, plants from fish and fowls and cattle, and now He comes to that epochal moment where He is about to create human life. In Genesis 1:26 we read the words of the Godhead, speaking together, "Let Us make man in Our image." Never before has such a statement appeared in Scripture, nor will it ever appear related to animal, plant, or any other life, including life that might be in the planetary spaces. This is limited to human life. Only human life—by God's design—possesses the image of God.

> Then God said, "Let Us make man in Our image, according to Our likeness; and let them rule over the fish of the sea and over the birds of the sky and over the cattle and over all the earth, and over every creeping thing that creeps on the earth." And God created man in His own image . . . (Gen. 1:26, 27).

As lovely, beautiful, colorful, and full of variety as the plant or animal kingdom may be, none of that has been created in God's image . . . only *human* life. Therefore (and it can be repeated time and again throughout Scripture), only human life can walk with and talk with and fellowship with the Creator. Animals cannot. Plants cannot. The fish cannot. *Only human beings* enjoy this privilege because only they possess God's image.

It should not surprise us, then, when we turn to Exodus 20:13, that we read, "You shall not murder." Why? Because there is something distinctly precious and unique about human life. In God's estimation, it is so precious and so unique He commands that it must be protected, it must be preserved. It alone represents "the image of God." This precious human life is not to be treated violently by other human beings. The One who creates life certainly has the right to appraise it. Simply speaking, it is God's way of saying, "Life is so important no one has the right to murder it. Don't end it. Let it live. Because all humanity represents My handiwork; it is Mine to do with as I please. My image is, in mysterious ways, stamped into human life."

If you think that is an exaggerated statement, listen to the psalmist.

> What is man, that Thou dost take thought of him: And the son of man, that Thou dost care for him? Yet Thou hast made him a little lower than God, and dost crown him with glory and majesty! (Psalm 8:4–5).

While I am not able to explain what all this means or declare the full spectrum of all it includes, I do know that such a statement is never made concerning an animal or a plant. As beautiful and full of variety as those creations are, neither of those categories has a glory and a majesty that is "a little lower than God." Such a statement is reserved only for human life.

Elsewhere, the psalmist writes that the Lord has been his God forever, even from his mother's womb:

> Yet Thou art He who didst bring me forth from the womb; Thou didst make me trust when upon my mother's breast. Upon Thee I was cast from birth; Thou hast been my God from my mother's womb (Psalm 22:9–10).

Look closely at those words. David is seeing himself within the womb and coming forth from it as being answerable to the God who created him and developed him during the nine months he was within the womb.

Did you know that the sin nature within the heart of human beings is present even within the life of the child in the womb? David says: "Behold, I was brought forth in iniquity, and in sin my mother conceived me" (Psalm 51:5). Some would read that and think, "Sounds to me like the act of sexual intercourse, the cause of his conception, was sinful." No, that is not what he meant. The Amplified Bible helps: "Behold, I was brought forth in [a state of] iniquity; my mother was sinful who conceived me [and I, too, am sinful]." One of the most capable linguistic authorities I have ever met—a Hebrew scholar *par excellence*—is Bruce Waltke (a Ph.D. from Harvard University) and one of my mentors during my seminary years. He writes of this Psalm 51:5 passage rather clearly, first quoting from Edward R. Dalglish's authoritative work on Psalm 51:

> In Psalm 51:5, the psalmist is relating his sinfulness to the very inception of life; he traces his development beyond his birth . . . to the genesis of his being in his mother's womb—even to the very hour of conception.[8]

Dr. Waltke then adds:

> . . . in tracing his spiritual condition to the time of conception, David goes on to note that already in his fetal state the moral law of God was present in him.[9]

Even in an embryonic or fetal state there was this sense of God's hand and God's accountability in the psalmist's life. This is vividly illustrated in the most eloquent passage supporting life in the womb in all the Old Testament: the central section of Psalm 139. I'm referring to verses 13–16.

> For Thou didst form my inward parts; Thou didst weave me in my mother's womb. I will give thanks to Thee, for I am fearfully and wonderfully made; wonderful are Thy works, and my soul knows it very well. My frame was not hidden from Thee, when I was made in secret, and skillfully wrought in the depths of the earth. Thine eyes have

seen my unformed substance; and in Thy book they were all written, the days that were ordained for me, when as yet there was not one of them.

It is as if the Spirit of God had taken a divine fiber-optic probe and reached into the womb, revealing the tender, all-powerful presence of God at work in the fetus.

> For Thou, [this is God] didst form my inward parts; Thou didst weave me in my mother's womb (v. 13).

His word picture describes the internal network of tiny organs that were formed by the Creator while the psalmist was in the womb of his mother.

Verse 15 mentions "my frame," clearly a reference to the bony structure, the skeleton, the bones, which would have to do with the height, the stature, the physique of the unborn child.

I wish time and space permitted me to describe the anatomical beauty, the variegated colors that are represented in the Hebrew words. It is pictured in the original language as if the bones and the arteries, the muscles and the structure of the body, are all divinely woven together. In addition, his personality was being designed along with other details like facial features, color of hair, and color of eyes, right down to toenails and fingernails, eyelashes and eyebrows. Small wonder he exclaims that he is "fearfully and wonderfully made"! Though tiny, the fetus receives God's careful attention.

Let me pause and summarize the three major points we have discovered thus far:

1. God sets apart human life as unique, distinctive, and valuable.

2. He therefore preserves and protects human life as no other life on earth.

3. That kind of life begins at conception and continues to develop in the womb where God is at work, shaping the child into the precise kind of person He desires it to be.

Moving into the New Testament, we come to the story of the Lord Jesus and His birth. Do you recall?

Now the birth of Jesus Christ was as follows. When His mother Mary had been betrothed to Joseph, before they came together she was found to be with child by the Holy Spirit. And Joseph her husband, being a righteous man, and not wanting to disgrace her, desired to put her away secretly. But when he had considered this, behold, an angel of the Lord appeared to him in a dream, saying, "Joseph, son of David, do not be afraid to take Mary as your wife; for that which has been conceived in her is of the Holy Spirit. And she will bear a Son; and you shall call His name Jesus, for it is He who will save

His people from their sins." Now all this took place
that what was spoken by the Lord through the
prophet might be fulfilled, saying, "BEHOLD, THE
VIRGIN SHALL BE WITH CHILD, AND SHALL
BEAR A SON, AND THEY SHALL CALL HIS
NAME IMMANUEL," which translated means,
"GOD WITH US" (Matt. 1:18–20).

Luke later mentions that what was being formed
in Mary, the mother of Jesus, was, in fact, "the holy
offspring" (Luke 1:35), not mere "fetal tissue." And
when Mary later stands before Elizabeth, her rela-
tive, and informs her that she is pregnant, do you
remember what occurred within Elizabeth, who was
also pregnant? "The baby leaped in her womb" (Luke
1:41). Blobs don't leap, neither do tissues and tu-
mors . . . only life leaps!

There is far too much scientific evidence to deny
that the fetus is, in fact, life . . . separate, independent, God-created life. Whether or not the
mother-to-be planned or expected to be pregnant
(Mary certainly didn't) she is carrying a life within
her that has as much right to live *before* birth as the
child does *after* birth.

Almost without exception today, the major part
of the argument is that the woman's rights take over
or have precedence over the life within her, as
though she were solely responsible for the conception of life within her. She is not . . . not really.
How often couples will have sexual relations again
and again and again with or without the use of

contraceptives—but there is no conception. And
then one day God sovereignly causes life to be conceived. The couple can no more say they had the
creative powers to begin that life within the woman
than they can say they have the final authority to
end it.

Well, you may be thinking, *what if her life is in
danger?* C. Everett Koop, M.D., formerly the Surgeon
General, states that during his 35-plus years of prac-
ticing medicine, "Never once did a case come across
my practice where abortion was necessary to save a
mother's life."[10] As we saw earlier in the statistics,
the percentage of such cases is so small, it is of negli-
gible concern for the use of argument.

I came across a rather interesting editorial cartoon several years ago. It was designed to make you
think, not laugh. It contained six frames of the same
woman.

First frame: "He kissed me and I
                 melted."

Second frame: "My heart pounded at his
                 touch."

Third frame: "His embrace sent the
                 blood coursing through
                 my veins."

Fourth frame: "I was overcome with
                 passion. I couldn't
                 refuse."

| Fifth frame: | "Well, now I'm pregnant and I want an abortion." |
| Last frame: | "After all, a woman should have control over her body." |

If there is irresponsibility prior to pregnancy, the chances are greatly increased there will be irresponsibility afterwards.

Just in case you are still not fully convinced that there is life within the womb, read this testimony of Paul E. Rockwell, M.D., slowly and carefully:

> Years ago, while giving an anesthetic for a ruptured tubal pregnancy (at two months), I was handed what I believed to be the smallest human being ever seen. The embryo sac was intact and transparent. Within the sac was a tiny (one-third inch) human male swimming extremely vigorously in the amniotic fluid, while attached to the wall by the umbilical cord. This tiny human was perfectly developed with long, tapering fingers, feet and toes. It was almost transparent as regards the skin, and the delicate arteries and veins were prominent to the ends of the fingers. The baby was extremely alive and did not look at all like the photos and drawings of "embryos" which I have seen. When the sac was opened, the tiny human immediately lost its life and took on the appearance of what is accepted as the appearance of an embryo at this stage, blunt extremities, etc.[11]

Perhaps I should pause here and state the logical syllogism that has emerged from Scripture:

First: God sets apart human life as unique and valuable since it bears His image.

Second: Because this is true, God commands that all human life be preserved and protected.

Third: Human life begins within the womb, where God personally and sovereignly superintends the development and maturation of the fetus before birth.

Fourth: Therefore, since it is God's will that every child's life be protected after birth, it is certainly His will that such protection apply to the child in his or her prenatal state.

The simple fact is this: Had your mother chosen not to have you at the time when she first became aware of your presence in her, you would not have known the joys you've had in life nor the privilege of growing to this present moment of your existence. For that matter, you would not be here reading these words and feeling those feelings you are experiencing at this moment. Thankfully, she determined you were worth whatever it took to give birth to you. Unfortunately, many are not making that decision today. Before you finish reading this book thousands of babies, permanently rejected by their mothers and fathers, will not be granted their God-given right to live, to laugh, to grow up, and to encounter the stimulating challenges of life. An abortion will bring all that to an abrupt and permanent end.

Some Suggestions That Call for Involvement

I am convinced that most who read this book are anxious to do something about abortion. But many of you are asking, "What?" I have seven suggestions, each of which calls for involvement.

First of all, volunteer your time, energy, and financial resources. There are several excellent organizations that are clearly pro-life who exist because people voluntarily help support them with time, energy, encouragement, and financial assistance.

Second, make your home available to unwed mothers and/or be of support to homes that are open to them. Give serious thought to this. You will discover, as my family and I did, that the small amount of privacy you may forfeit will seem insignificant in comparison to the investment you will make in another's life and future.

Third, write letters and make phone calls. Get involved as a citizen in your local government and in the lives of those in national leadership who make a difference, especially those who are making a difference in legislation.

Fourth, participate in demonstrations of your personal preference. More and more are convinced that this is what they should do. Some in the church I pastor have chosen to participate in Operation Rescue or some other form of peaceful demonstration. Others have participated in public rallies and marches, declaring their disagreement with the proabortion activists. This is not for everyone, but it is for many. It may be for you. It may not be. But don't decide to do *nothing* because one particular method of public expression is not for you. Find something that is.

Fifth, participate in community projects. More than ever, neighborhoods are organizing projects that make a statement to the whole city. Be open to the possibility of your participating in that.

Sixth, practice in your private life what you claim to believe publicly. Model moral purity. Abstain from extramarital sexual involvements. If you find that you are pregnant, accept what God chooses for you whether or not you planned it or expected it. Another thought along the lines of doing something publicly you claim to believe privately . . . seriously consider adopting. I know, I know, it's a major decision, but what a statement it makes! Furthermore, just imagine the fulfillment of loving and influencing a child who might otherwise know nothing of the joy you could bring into his or her life.

To encourage you even more, consider the words of a fourteen-year-old boy named Jason who expresses these thoughts to his adoptive parents.

Once when I was a lot younger I watched a television show on abortion. I saw how many thousands of women were aborting their babies before they were born. I remember how glad I was that my biological mother chose to carry me and my twin brother Josh to full term and give birth. Then she let us be adopted into a wonderful family. I might not even be here today, except that my biological mother loved me enough to let me be born. And my new family loved me enough to make a wonderful home for me.

A lot of people think adoption is a bad thing. They think maybe the parents that adopt you wouldn't love you as much as their own kids. Sometimes this may be true, but in my family it is not.

When my parents adopted me, they took a big risk. They knew in my biological family there was a problem called dyslexia, a severe reading disability. They also knew there was diabetes in my biological family. I was born with one foot turned in, and I had to have surgery to correct an indentation in my skull. My parents knew they would need to give me special attention. Knowing all this they still wanted Josh and me, even though twins are twice the work. My mom and dad didn't care that Josh and I were black and they were white. They loved us just the way we were.

One good thing about adoption is I always know I was really loved and wanted, because I was chosen. When I get to be 18, I know I could look for my biological parents, but I would not. I already have a loving and caring mom and dad. Adoption is the greatest gift in life to me.[12]

Seventh, pray, pray, pray, and PRAY! Pray for those who are on the front lines of the battle. Pray for the politicians, the pastors, the physicians, the ministers, pro-life leaders in the media, and those who lead anti-abortion organizations, all of whom face incredible pressure. Write them and assure them of your prayers. Last, but certainly not least, pray for the mothers-to-be . . . that more and more will be courageous and choose against abortion.

I close this chapter with a true story. A couple married during the Great Depression. The man was middle-aged, and the woman was in her mid-twenties. Before they had been married a year, in fact, exactly ten months after their wedding day, God gave them their first child—a boy. It was difficult, but in spite of their financial restraints they handled it fairly well. Before they had been married two years, along came a second child—an infant girl. Lo and behold, in January, long before their fourth anniversary the following October, the mother conceived her third child, even though they were using a contraceptive. The other two children were still in diapers.

It was a tremendously difficult time for this couple financially. The mother's health was not good and her energy level, understandably, was at an all-time low. Furthermore, she was not all that great with young children. She was depressed. Their financial burden was enormous . . . perhaps so enormous they could have been tempted to seek the help of someone who would perform an abortion.

The time was early 1934, an era when abortions were illegal. However, the woman and her husband were convinced that they should accept whatever God sovereignly had planned for them. Sacrificially, they chose to have that baby—a boy—who was born in October of that year.

I'm so grateful that they did, because I was that baby, my mother and father's last child. Our family came to know a joy in family life that the five of us would otherwise never have known. Little did anyone realize back then what God's plan for me would have been. Today, all three of my parents' children are engaged in vocational Christian service.

I am more grateful than I can describe that my mother and father, both now deceased, agreed: "We'll have you, because we believe God is greater than our plans and our rights. We believe God's plan, though mysterious, is far more magnificent and important than a few inconveniences." Because they thought those thoughts many years ago, I am able to write these things today.

2

Abortion . . .
after the Fact

You might wonder how anyone could choose to have an abortion after reading what you just read in the previous chapter. The harsh reality, the scriptural facts, the undeniable statistics, and the sheer logic may seem formidable enough to restrain anyone from deciding to kill a helpless fetus. But whoever thinks that isn't being realistic. Apart from church congregations and organizations that promote the pro-life position, this persuasion is not reflected in most high-profile settings.

How easy for mothers-to-be to weaken when clear-thinking logic is removed. How easy for a woman to panic and opt for a "quick fix," even though she may know intellectually that her decision lacks biblical or moral justification. The fact is, some decisions are made quite shortsightedly.

And when you think about it from her perspective, there really are many occasions when a woman could talk herself into an abortion. I am thinking of an intelligent, competent 31-year-old career woman who has been offered her long-awaited dream in life, a management position that shows great promise. It shouldn't take her too many years to hit the big time. She is sexually active, but she is not married. Three weeks after she has accepted the job of her lifetime, she discovers that she is pregnant. She is not ready either for marriage or for a child. Maternity leave is out of the question if she hopes to proceed with her new career. Too many adjustments . . . the boss couldn't handle it. To make matters worse, her sexual partner urges her to escape all the hassle, "Get an abortion. I'll pay for the whole thing," he reasons. It makes good sense. Her future is on the line. She is all alone, away from her family. It will be so quick and absolutely private; no one would ever know. It's nobody else's business, anyway. Not surprisingly, she takes him up on his offer.

Another case would be the 17-year-old high school senior who lets her passions get away from her on a winter weekend at a ski retreat. Shocked, she discovers in February before graduation in June that she is going to have a baby. Her parents will never understand. His won't either. The teenaged girl is confused beyond description. Her boyfriend thinks that there is a way he may be able to scrape up enough money to help her with this problem. She thinks of trying to be a mother at eighteen or living with the stigma of an illegitimate child. Maybe she could slip away to some home and have the baby away from her familiar surroundings. But that would mean she wouldn't graduate. Furthermore, she can kiss her university scholarship good-bye. Her boyfriend shows up with the money. He tells her he will drive her to the clinic and be there when it's all over. She yields—naturally.

Or what about the 39-year-old mother of five whose husband has recently left her? It's New Year's Eve. She has too much to drink and spends the night with a guy she met at the party. After one sexual encounter she gets pregnant. The last thing she wants is another child. She can barely make it financially as it is . . . and now she learns that she is going to have another mouth to feed. To her the best answer is something she would not normally consider. After all, she is a fairly responsible single parent. But she has read the literature and listened to other ladies at work who lived through an abortion. "No problem, Doris. You just found out you're pregnant. All the doctor will do is remove some fetal tissue and before you know it, you're back on your feet. Be smart." That settled it.

My hope in this chapter is to look at the other

side of what I wrote earlier. I want to help others to understand what it must be like to make a decision like I have just described in a moment of panic and fear. I also want to underscore the harsh realities of what can happen after the fact. What seemed like a quick fix isn't that at all. How often women who chose to get an abortion look back on it years later and feel the horror, the regret in making a decision that seemed right at the moment but now, in light of the passing of years, it represents the low-water mark of their past. The shame is frequently so overwhelming; deep depression and thoughts of suicide won't go away.

In this chapter I want to write to you who have had an abortion. I hope my words will help you. I also write to you who have aided in an abortion medically . . . or have encouraged someone you love to have an abortion, thinking it would help, and you realize now it did not.

A Story Worth Everyone's Attention

Bill Hybels, senior pastor of Willow Creek Community Church in Barrington, Illinois, a suburb of Chicago, has written a fine booklet entitled *One Church's Answer to Abortion.* In it, this fine minister relates a touching story, followed by counsel that is worth everyone's attention.

I've talked to many women who say to me, "Please tell the truth to the women of the church. Abortion is not a quick fix. What accompanies the

'quick fix' may very well be a lifetime of regret—
shadows, sinister thoughts, crippling dreams, and
nightmares." There are articles published almost
monthly under such titles as "Paying the Price of
Abortion" or "The Child I Will Never See." But you
don't hear that kind of counsel coming from abortion clinic counselors.

Before I spoke on this topic in church, I received
this note from a man: "When I heard you were going
to speak on the topic of abortion, I just knew I had to
write to you. This topic has crippled me more than
any other subject. Right out of high school I got my
girl friend pregnant. I insisted that she get an abortion. There's a hundred reasons I could give why
I took the actions I did, but they would all be lies. I
settled for the quick fix—the easy way of avoiding
the embarrassment of being found out. And you
know what? That was a lie too. Yes, it avoided some
embarrassment, but it was replaced by a different
type of pain. The pain of remorse. Each spring when
life is starting to bloom, there's a renewed pain that
my child could be adding another year. . . ."

Through genuine repentance, anyone can re-
ceive forgiveness from God. It is a marvelous healing gift to be claimed by everyone. But in my next
breath I have to say that even though you are forgiven before God, you may still see and feel some
scars. Don't buy the lie that a quick fix has no long-
term effects.

Little is said about the emotional trauma that
accompanies an abortion, and seldom are warnings
given about the medical complications that often

come as a result of an abortion. Statistics show that after an abortion has been performed, a woman faces increased possibility of future miscarriages, tubal pregnancies, premature births, and sterility.

Seldom will an abortion clinic counselor show prenatal pictures to a woman considering an abortion. If the baby can be referred to as tissue, it's much easier to avoid any emotional attachment to it. But what would the results be if women were shown ultrasound pictures of a twelve-week-old baby who is kicking, curling his toes, rotating his feet and wrists, and making facial expressions? Most women would not abort babies—tissue masses maybe—but not babies. Abortion procedures are too gruesome to contemplate when the object is a baby.[13]

A Desire for Understanding

In this second chapter, my hope is for understanding.

First, I want you to understand me. I am not soft on abortion. If you start to doubt that, just return to the things I wrote in the previous chapter. Nothing I write in this chapter is designed to take the edge off what I wrote earlier. My hope is to bring a needed balance between what could easily have come off earlier as uncaring, cold, and statistical. That was never my intention. But sometime when I feel passionate about a subject, my zeal for truth can overshadow my compassion for the hurting. My hope is to communicate in this chapter the possibility of full recovery and a return to a life that is productive, fruitful, and free of guilt.

Second, I want the person who has had an abortion (or advised someone else to do so) to have an understanding of God's response. Life not only can . . . it must go on. We live in an imperfect world. Disobedience happens on a daily basis. To require perfection of others or of ourselves is going too far. If I have learned anything in these three decades I have spent in the pastorate, it is that sin happens on a regular basis. In others' lives and in my own life, disobedience occurs. Irresponsible actions following bad decisions take place even among good and wise people. And when it does, what I have discovered is the last person we are willing to forgive is ourselves. Most of us are readily willing to forgive another individual, certainly upon confession and repentance, but though we may confess and repent of our own wrongdoing, we put ourselves under such a cloud of shame, we enter into unproductive years by refusing to take God at His Word and accept His full forgiveness. My desire is that the person who has made a regrettable decision and acted independently of God's counsel will find hope to go on. There is a tomorrow.

General Facts from God's Relevant Word

I want to draw from the Scripture four statements that you can know for a fact, that you can rely on and ultimately act on. These facts are not limited to the sin of abortion, but they certainly would include it.

Fact one: *Sin is sin, and we all commit it.* The categories are numerous and the reasons we do these sins are also numerous. In its most basic sense, sin is missing the mark. It is failing to obey the truth. According to God's Book, all of us are guilty:

> For all have sinned and fall short of the glory of God (Rom. 3:23).

Every person who will ever read my words knows the personal reality and agony of that verse. All of us indeed have sinned. Even the godly, the righteous, the well-meaning will periodically sin. Not until we are removed from this earth, glorified, and ushered into the presence of our Lord in eternity after death will we stop sinning. As long as we are in existence, breath is in our lungs, and life is on this planet, we will continue to disobey. That means every one of us.

> The Lord has looked down from heaven upon the sons of men, to see if there are any who understand, who seek after God. They have all turned aside; together they have become corrupt; there is no one who does good, not even one (Psalm 14:2–3).

If I may paraphrase it, certainly it would have in mind, "There is no one who continually and without interruption does only good." We all know the awful experience of failure and wrong and disobedience. It is long-term in all our lives.

> The wicked are estranged from the womb; these who speak lies go astray from birth (Psalm 58:3).

I hold our precious little grandchildren in my arms and I look into their adorable, cupidlike faces and I have to force myself to remember that each one is a sinner. As a grandfather, I find that a little difficult to believe . . . until we baby-sit, then I know each one has a very strong will. Behind that adorable face and that precious life is a nature that is estranged from God since each one was born. They may begin life as sweet, innocent infants, but it isn't long before they demonstrate a sinful nature. Interestingly, no child ever needs to be taught how to disobey. We all sin. We have. We do. We shall. Sin is sin. And we've all committed it.

Fact two: *God is grieved but never surprised or shocked by our disobedience.*

> As far as the east is from the west, so far has He removed our transgressions from us. Just as a father has compassion on his children, so the Lord has compassion on those who fear Him. For He Himself knows our frame; He is mindful that we are but dust (Psalm 103:12–14).

When God holds us in His arms, looking deeply into our faces, and sees our tears of repentance, regret, sadness, and sorrow, He understands. He sees behind the beauty of our gifts and beyond the contribution of our lives as He acknowledges the reality of our sins. He hears our confessions. And without once winking at our sins or passing them off glibly, He understands our makeup. He remembers that we are mere dust.

I've often thought of the great contrast within gifted, great lives. We hear beautiful music from those talented and capable people who studied for years and perfected their gifts to such an extent, they are able to play or sing magnificent music. How easy to forget that within those very same lives are the grossest seeds of what could be the most heinous crimes and acts of depravity. Crimes of enormous passion could be committed by any one of those gifted people. And even with them, God fully understands . . . which means He is willing to forgive.

Sin is sin. It happens regularly. And when it happens, God is grieved . . . but He is not shocked.

Fact three: *Some sins incur greater consequences than others.* Yes, sin is sin, but not all sins lead to the same consequences. Some sins are private, unknown, and impact no one other than the person who committed them. You deal with them and they are secretly confessed and swiftly forgiven, never to hurt another soul. It happens daily. Other sins are public and become known, which means they impact many. There are still other sins that are of a criminal nature. They are crimes against society. Those can result in public embarrassment, financial penalty, a loss of reputation, and a sentence behind bars, not to mention the humiliation of the family and the loss of respect in the eyes of the public. While some sins are unknown, other sins are scandalous and shameful, hurtful to our own spirit, and damaging to our health. It is also possible for us to be involved in a mixture of any and all the above.

Let me show you from Scripture an example of the kind of sins that bears greater consequences. Proverbs 5 mentions the sin of adultery.

> For why should you, my son, be exhilarated with an adulteress, and embrace the bosom of a foreigner? For the ways of a man are before the eyes of the Lord, and He watches all his paths. His own iniquities will capture the wicked, and he will be held with the cords of his sin. He will die for lack of instruction, and in the greatness of his folly he will go astray (Prov. 5:20–23).

The vivid imagery of the writer's style pictures it as though there were tentacles that reach around a person and bind him with "the cords of his sin." The complications and consequences of adultery are discussed even further in the next chapter of Proverbs:

> Can a man take fire in his bosom, and his clothes not be burned? Or can a man walk on hot coals, and his feet not be scorched? So is the one who goes in to his neighbor's wife; whoever touches her will not go unpunished (Prov. 6:27–29).

And then:

> The one who commits adultery with a woman is lacking sense; he who would destroy himself does it. Wounds and disgrace he will find, and his reproach will not be blotted out (Prov. 6:32–33).

Under the general category of sexual sins or immorality there is a lingering consequence or series of consequences that are inescapable. The scars remain. Sexually related sins are in a category unto themselves in Scripture. If the following statement says anything, it certainly suggests that thought:

> Flee immorality. Every other sin that a man commits is outside the body, but the immoral man sins against his own body (1 Cor. 6:18).

(We'll consider this statement more in depth in Chapter 3.)

Yes, sin is sin. While it may grieve God, it doesn't shock Him. He understands and is willing to forgive. Forgiven or not, there are some sins that have lingering effects. Those sins can create within us and others an extremely lengthy and sad series of consequences. David admits to this in his thirty-second psalm.

> When I kept silent about my sin, my body wasted away through my groaning all day long. For day and night Thy hand was heavy upon me; my vitality was drained away as with the fever-heat of summer (Psalm 32:3).

He is describing the guilt that came in the backwash of his affair with Bathsheba. In the clutches of the vice-grip guilt put on him, he tossed and turned on his bed. He churned within. He couldn't escape the lingering horror of what he had done.

I have met women who speak of similar feelings after they had an abortion. The event may be over but the "groaning" lingers.

A couple of summers ago I was engaged in ministry at Mount Hermon Christian Conference Center up near Santa Cruz. It was our annual Insight for Living family camp. After I had spoken one morning we showed a film dealing with the facts of an abortion. We realized that there might be some who could be impacted by what was presented. Our hope was that we would capture the attention of the naive as well as inform those who were ignorant of the facts and perhaps even reach some who might be teetering on the edge of this very decision.

One young woman, after viewing the film, could hardly move. She dissolved in tears. As you would guess, she had had an abortion. What was interesting, and perhaps a bit surprising to some, her abortion had occurred several years earlier. But the reminder of what had happened and of what had been done with the life that had been taken, was almost more than she could bear. She sat there virtually immobile and sobbing, reliving the events of what had long since passed. She admitted that a "cycle of depression" periodically overcame her, which began shortly after she had the abortion.

Sin is sin. God is grieved. But some sins incur lengthy consequences. There is still that recurring cycle of grief and depression, which does not automatically go away.

As Nathan said to David in 2 Samuel 12, "You

are forgiven, but the sword will never depart from your house." (Think of that!) And indeed it didn't. David's life had changed from a little shepherd lad on the Judean hillsides to his becoming the king of the Hebrew nation. But when Bathsheba came on the scene, life for him was never quite the same. In his own words, he entered into the "fever heart of summer."

Fact four: *Recovery and return to a fruitful life is God's desire for all of us.* Just as there is not an earthly father who desires to discipline a son and leave him in a state of discipline for the rest of their relationship, so our heavenly Father, though He disciplines us and brings us to brokenness, has no interest in our living out our lives under the constant severity of His discipline. Discipline happens for a period of time and then God's grace comes to our rescue, giving us fruitfulness and purpose as we go on beyond the immobilizing impact of the guilt and shame of our failure.

But the question is how. What is needed to go on with one's life after gross failure before God and others? For the sake of clarity and brevity, let me list a four-step process that will help you get back on your feet. What is needed?

1. *A full acknowledgment of the wrong that was done.*

If we confess our sins, He is faithful and righteous to forgive us our sins and to cleanse us from all unrighteousness (1 John 1:9).

Have you fully acknowledged the wrong of your past? If not, take care of that now. No more defensiveness. No more excuses. No more human reasoning or logic, trying to convince yourself otherwise. Rather, a full and complete acknowledgment of the wrong of your action is needed. God honors such submissiveness. I understand the word confession to mean that we agree with God in every respect that the sin was wrong, and it is without excuse or defense.

2.   *Genuine repentance following the confession.*

Not much is said or heard these days about repentance. Too bad. It is a necessary part of finding full relief from guilt's bondage. Genuine repentance follows confession. Proverbs 28:13 states:

> He who conceals his transgressions will not prosper, but he who confesses and forsakes them will find compassion.

This refers to a full and complete forsaking of the act, a turning around in the mind, a reversal of emotions. Repentance is a change of reaction from defense to a full acknowledgment. From an attempt to excuse one's sin to an absolute and unguarded realization and admission that the whole of it was wrong, accompanied with a desire never to repeat it.

Psalm 51 is of great help in this context because it has to do with sexual failure.

> Be gracious to me, O God, according to Thy lovingkindness; according to the greatness of Thy compassion blot out my transgressions. Wash me thoroughly from my iniquity, and cleanse me from my sin. For I know my transgressions, and my sin is ever before me. Against Thee, Thee only, I have sinned, and done what is evil in Thy sight, so that Thou art justified when Thou dost speak, and blameless when Thou dost judge (Psalm 51:1–4).

There is no sense of "How could You do this to me, God?" But rather, "I acknowledge Your right to do whatever You wish. I deserve nothing but judgment. I am at Your mercy, Lord. I come with a contrite heart." We cannot help but be impressed with the attitude as well as the words of the psalmist.

Psalm 51 continues:

> Restore to me the joy of Thy salvation, and sustain me with a willing spirit. Then I will teach transgressors Thy ways, and sinners will be converted to Thee. O Lord, open my lips, that my mouth may declare Thy praise. For Thou dost not delight in sacrifice, otherwise I would give it; Thou art not pleased with burnt offering. The sacrifices of God are a broken spirit; a broken and a contrite heart, O God, Thou wilt not despise (vv. 12–13).

There is a difference between remorse and repentance. Remorse is sorrow over being caught, sadness brought on by the pain of the consequences, the humiliation of the loss of image and the feeling,

"What will people say?" Remorseful feelings include knowing that you have brought reproach on the name of a family or on a church, or on your own life. But in genuine repentance, we lose all concern for ourselves, we accept the humiliation that we deserve and we acknowledge the grief we have caused others. The tell-tale signs? A broken spirit and a contrite heart.

Please understand me here. My concern is not to make anyone do penance but to make certain that genuine confession is accompanied by genuine repentance. An abortion is a serious offense before God, but it is not unforgivable. God stands ready to forgive . . . but the process involved can be heartrending: confessing, repenting, forsaking. I don't know how and I don't know why these things are so effective . . . I just know that they represent God's pattern.

3. *In the process, we claim the cleansing God offers.*

We've seen it again and again through this passage in Psalm 51. As we work through the process, we can lay claim to the cleansing God offers. The references are numerous:

"Wash me thoroughly . . . cleanse
    me . . ." (v. 2).
"Purify me . . . and I shall be clean;
    wash me, and I shall be whiter than
    snow (v. 7).

"Create in me a clean heart, O God . . ."
(v. 10).

"Restore to me the joy of Thy salvation,
and sustain me with a willing spirit"
(v. 12).

"Then I will teach transgressors Thy ways,
and sinners will be converted to Thee"
(v. 13).

I've found that God often uses forgiven individuals to assist others. It is called here "teaching transgressors Thy ways." I ask you: Who is better able to minister to those who are tempted to get an abortion than those who have had one? Who is better able to describe the consequences than those who have suffered through them? These dreadful experiences, in the words of Scripture, enable you to teach others God's way. What a great opportunity to minister to people when we work our way through the process of full cleansing which follows full forgiveness!

Maybe you've never thought of it before, but those who have gone through an abortion and found forgiveness and cleansing might be on the verge of a ministry you never dreamed possible.

4. *Deliberately refuse to allow the adversary or anyone else to hold you in bondage to former sins.*

I need to be painfully honest here. Some need help to work through this process. Yes, some need a paid, professional Christian counselor to assist them through the therapy of recovery. Others may need a pastor. Most certainly a support group is needed. And who can deny the need for a friend to help us talk and walk our way through so that we sense God's full cleansing and full forgiveness? Once relief comes, no one has a right to hold a woman back and put her on a guilt trip. My point is clear: It isn't uncommon to need direct assistance to get beyond nightmares and shadows of past wrongs. Ultimately, it may alter the direction of your future, but it doesn't mean you are finished, washed up, and shelved. And don't let anyone hold you under the bondage of forgiven sins from which you have repented. God's desire is that you go on with the rest of your life.

Advice to All Who Live with Regret

May I conclude this chapter with some pastoral advice and compassionate counsel? First, *you cannot undo the past; don't try.* I meet folks rather regularly who think that if they travel far enough and long enough the travel will cause them to erase the past. Wasted effort. Not even an around-the-world trip will help you absolve your past. Drugs won't do it either. Alcohol won't do it. Finding a marriage partner won't necessarily remove what has been done in the past. It certainly will soften the blow of it as you walk with God, but you cannot undo what has been done. You cannot unscramble an egg. God alone is your only Source of relief.

Second, *you may not be able to cope with the present; don't quit.* Some folks have a whale of a battle on their hands. If you are one of them, I commend you for not quitting. Get help. Go back to the third statement I gave you earlier. Work through the process of finding full forgiveness methodically and carefully. Don't hold anything back. It might include going to individuals whom you hurt or offended or wronged in some way. It may be that your abortion represents only a part of your problem. Stay at it until you are free. Being unable to cope simply means the process isn't complete. Don't quit.

Third and finally, *you must not waste the future; don't hide.* I do not believe that God gives anyone breath in his or her lungs for the purpose of just existing. God has a purpose for every one of us. He is well able to remake and reshape your life. I am a firm believer in second chances. If we are going to say with full faith to people who have gone through the horrors of divorce, "there is a future," then I must say to you who have gone through the sin and humiliation of an abortion, there is a future for you, too! I repeat, God has a purpose. And it is not that you spend your days in hiding.

May He grant you a special measure of grace . . . grace to face the truth, painful though it may be. Grace to accept His forgiveness, unworthy though you may feel. And grace to become one of His choice instruments, impossible though that may seem. God isn't finished with you yet.

His grace is abundant. Claim it. It is the map that will lead you to the promised land of a full and complete recovery.

3

A Plea for Morality

Every person reading these words is married. You have a companion who will be with you for life. Every morning, as sure as the rising of the sun, your partner is there. Every evening, immutable as the arrival of darkness, your companion is still by your side. This companion will never leave you because of lack of support or incompatibility . . . and a divorce is impossible. You and your partner are married forever, till death do you part.

Your partner, your lifelong companion, is temptation.

There is no escape, no immunity, no exemption, and no relief. Even if you entered into the role of the priesthood and lived the balance of your life behind the thick walls of a monastery, your battle would go on; your companion would be there, taunting you and haunting you almost on a daily basis.

This is nothing new; it's been going on for centuries. Because temptation feeds on our curiosity, it continues to tell us what we don't have and what we ought to have. Because it depends upon comparison, it keeps whispering the age-old lie that the grass is greener on the other side of the fence. It never runs out of carrots, telling you that something or someone is better than what you have and it is worth the risk; yield, and you will find satisfaction. This is nothing new. This is not a late century-twenty malady.

An Ancient Scene with a Relevant Ring

Step into the time tunnel with me and travel back 3,000 years ago. The nation is Israel. The city is Jerusalem. The season is spring. The time is evening. And the hour is early. The place is the roof of the king's palace. It is a quiet evening. A soft breeze blows across the city. And in a rare moment of unaccountable privacy and relaxation, the king is walking on the roof to find some solitude in the cool evening breeze.

Beyond the palace lives a young married woman. No children. Her husband is away in military service.

She is the daughter of Eliam . . . the wife of Uriah. In unguarded innocence, she is taking an evening bath. She is not a sultry, cheap streetwalker, or a sexually frustrated woman. She is a faithful wife. And the man who stops to watch her? He is around forty years of age . . . a dignified, respected monarch. He's a gallant warrior, handsome and gifted, not a sex-starved peeping Tom. He has at least seven wives, not to mention several concubines. He has fathered seventeen children. Clearly, he is not some kind of prowling human animal in heat. He had two dangerous possessions, however—time on his hands and an evening of unaccountable privacy. No question, he is attracted. He cannot take his eyes off her.

In her novel *David and Bathsheba,* Roberta Dorr portrays it vividly.

Bathsheba pulled off her shift and stepped into the alabaster bowl her servant Sarah had filled with fresh water. She stood naked in the bowl while her servant dipped water with a gourd and poured it over her. Bathsheba stood without embarrassment even though she had nothing to cover her nakedness. Unknown to her, a man's eyes had been observing and . . . ordinarily he would have turned away, but it was all so unexpected and lovely that he continued to watch. With growing admiration, he studied her loveliness as only half-seen through the the dried palm branches. Her hair clung in damp curls to her full breasts and her tiny waist accentuated the pleasing roundness of her hips. As he watched, she stepped out of the bowl and tossed her hair back, making the curve of her back visible. He thought he'd never seen anything so beautiful or so graceful in his life.[14]

A quiet rap on her door later that evening changed her plans not only for the rest of the night but for the rest of her life.

Understand that up until this encounter David and Bathsheba had never met. If he had met her, she was one among many in the streets of Jerusalem who had bowed before the king. He didn't even know her name. But before that night was over, she would have his child within her.

Let's understand right away that illicit sex is neither novel nor new. It is not something that has grown out of today's society. Sexual temptation has been a part of humanity throughout time. As I stated at the beginning of the chapter, it is a marriage from which there is no escape. Chapter 1 of the New Testament letter of James describes in clear and brief terms a downward cycle that is taken by all who taste of temptation's forbidden fruit:

> Let no one say when he is tempted, "I am being tempted by God"; for God cannot be tempted by evil, and He Himself does not tempt any one. But each one is tempted when he is carried away and enticed by his own lust (James 1:13–14).

An Analysis of Lust's Allurement

Since it is fairly easy to analyze sexual temptation in a safe place such as that in which we find ourselves at this moment—a book open in your lap, lights are bright . . . no soft music . . . no sultry temptress in front of you—let's do so. So let's get real objective. This is a splendid opportunity to analyze how it all happens, how the secret, smoldering fire can burst into a destructive blaze that ruins a reputation, a career, a home, and finally a life.

While thinking about this in these recent days, I have come up with some simple terms that describe how and why this kind of thing happens.

As I think through the whole nine yards of sensual temptations, I find that there are several steps downward. First, there is an innocent *attraction.* Nothing wrong with that. Almost without exception, it is nothing more than a spontaneous observation. God has given us bodies. One person notices another. Some people have beautiful bodies, wonderful shapes and figures, and they keep themselves well attired. There is nothing wrong with that. In fact, it is commendable. Furthermore, the enjoyment of the beauty of another individual is not in itself sin. It occurs every day without evil intentions. We even compliment others who are not our marriage partners because we think they look nice. It is a courteous expression meant in sincerity and interpreted the same way. It is nothing more than an innocent attraction, but it's a start.

Second, this innocent attraction leads to what we might call *curiosity.* Webster defines it, "a desire to know, interest leading to inquiry." There is a desire to know more about the other person, which prompts further inquiry. At this point, mental comparisons usually take place. While getting to know another individual of the opposite sex, it is a great temptation to compare that person to someone else, often the one we're married to. And invariably we find things that are missing in our partner. Men are especially vulnerable at this point. Our expectations are often unrealistic. As I heard one woman say recently, "I'm expected today to be Mother Teresa, Margaret Thatcher, Chris Evert, and Cheryl Ladd all wrapped up in one. And all I really am is Betty Crocker."

The fire of comparison is fueled by increased curiosity. The one whom we do not know intimately is secretly compared to the one we know extremely well, and we see something lacking . . . *invariably* something is lacking.

Third, the door of curiosity opens the way to guarded *imagination.* I don't believe sin has occurred at this point. Temptation happens all the time. But it is at this juncture that our imagination is triggered as it begins to play a vital role. By the time the next step is taken, sin has occurred.

The fourth step downward is *fantasy.* Fantasy is the free play of one's creative and uninhibited imagination. Fantasy is mixing desires and wishes with dreams that are usually held in restraint. If unrestrained, the fantasy playground of the mind is capable of picturing the most intimate sexual activity with a person who was once nothing more than an attractive acquaintance.

Finally, this leads to a *full-scale lust.* Lust is an overpowering desire to enter into the actual fulfillment of one's fantasy. When lust takes charge, normal restraints are removed. I can think of four restraints that are blown to the winds at this point.

1.   Ignoring one's personal reputation, commitment, and moral standard. Lust cancels out those personal things. All of us have certain things that serve to encourage personal purity. It is those things that lust removes from our minds.

A man who had had a marvelous ministry for many years told me that when he fell into an affair with another woman, it got to where he could hardly remember he was married and was occasionally unable to name his own children. Another said it got to where he was so addicted to the other woman that when he was sexually intimate with his wife he felt he was unfaithful to his mistress. That is how twisted things get.

2.   Blindness to the consequences. You don't think about this tearing up your career. You don't consider how some will find out and how the thing will bring heartbreak to your children and grandchildren. Again, lust cancels out all those consequences.

3.   Not surprisingly, wrong is rationalized. You begin to tell yourself lies. Dark becomes light. The questionable becomes acceptable. Rationalization breaks down clear-thinking logic.

4. There is a burning excitement to proceed, no matter what. Whoever reaches that point of no return *cannot* stop. The excitement reaches such a fever pitch, all restraint is tossed to the winds.

I had an interesting experience in January of 1990. I had been invited to speak in New Orleans at the Super Bowl breakfast sponsored by Athletes in Action. En route from Los Angeles to New Orleans, I had to change planes in another city. The connecting flight was packed, naturally, and there was a festive spirit on board since everyone was headed for Super Bowl XXIV. I noticed an empty seat behind mine . . . the only empty seat on the plane. Only minutes before we backed away from the terminal, one final passenger hurried on board. Her plane had been late arriving, making it questionable if she could make her New Orleans connection. She did. As she hurried on, a bit harried, she immediately broke into a broad smile as her eyes met those of the man sitting next to the seat she would occupy. She didn't simply sit down—she fell into his arms as they kissed, giggled, and embraced for the next ten minutes.

My immediate thought was, *Now there's a happily married couple!* How wrong I was. They were both married . . . but not to each other. Because they sat right behind me, I got the full scoop. I must confess to some eavesdropping. Their carefully arranged plan was to rendezvous on the plane, then spend the weekend together in New Orleans. Their conversation, mixed with frequent kisses, included all kinds of comments about the fun they had in front of them, the intimate ecstasy of being together for a couple of nights, along with attending the Super Bowl. Both laughed and joked together as they talked about how each other's mate knew nothing of it. I might add here that neither made any mention of the possible consequences—the loss of reputation, of the depression that was sure to follow, the possibility of an unexpected pregnancy, the embarrassing humiliation when their mates (not if, but when) would find out. Why, of course not! This couple was on fire. Their full focus turned to the delightful time they would have together. They just couldn't talk about anything else.

All the while I'm sitting there in front of them, working on this chapter on sexual temptation, thirty-six inches behind me is a living illustration of lust in action. There flashed through my mind these words Solomon once wrote: "Stolen waters are sweet." No doubt about it. Unbridled, blinding lust is running over with the sweet-tasting ecstasy of sensual pleasure—at least for a weekend. Laughter, creativity, and excitement abound in such sexual escapades. It is not until later that the fog lifts and reality returns with its Monday-morning depression.

Strangely, an affair seldom stops with one encounter. More often than not, it is followed by another . . . and another. Frequently, babies are conceived who aren't wanted. Once lust has taken charge, a defense mechanism goes into action: protect yourself, blame others or circumstances, and

eliminate the evidence . . . which, being interpreted, means "get an abortion."

Back in the days of David's affair, that wasn't an
option. Such an abortion was, in fact, out of the
question. When Bathsheba informed the king of her
pregnancy, his defense mechanism led to deception,
hypocrisy, and finally murder. All this culminated
in an unending series of family heartaches and
tragedies brought on by divine judgment. Today it is
easier: *just kill the baby* and go on. It's a quick 'n'
dirty birth control method—if you don't mind
killing babies.

It's exactly as James 1:15 describes the final
scene: "death." Lust gives birth to sin. When sin is
accomplished, there is a strange kind of aborted ecstasy that leaves you with a twisted mind, a broken
relationship in the bond you once had in your marriage, and the beginning of the seeds dropped for a
sexual addiction that you won't be able to stop. In
short, it is living death.

Three Significant Scriptures
with Practical Warnings

Because temptations such as I have been describing
will never go away, it is essential to be prepared.
One of the most effective methods of preparation is
an awareness of what the Bible teaches, followed by
a direct and personal application of those truths.
Inevitably, there will come other unaccountable
times of personal privacy, times of temptation when
you are alone, when you are in a place that you

thought was safe, like David on his roof. It was true of the king. In reality, it could prove to be the most dangerous place of your life. Perhaps these three significant scriptures will be helpful in keeping you morally pure.

First Thessalonians 4. Of all Paul's writings, this is perhaps his most explicit statement regarding moral purity. As you will see, the information is not complicated. The explanation is not deep and mysterious. And the ultimate command, for sure, is not impossible.

The first two verses seem to be saying, *"In your walk, please God by excelling."*

> Finally then, brethren, we request and exhort you in the Lord Jesus, that, as you received from us instruction as to how you ought to walk and please God (just as you actually do walk), that you may excel still more. For you know what commandments we gave you by the authority of the Lord Jesus (1 Thess. 4:1–2).

God would have us go further and further in our walk with Him. Each day it pleases Him to make sure our goals are high, our desires are great, our objective is clear. He says, "Excel in that. As you walk, please God by excelling. Don't be satisfied with just a mediocre lifestyle as a Christian. Work on personal holiness. Cultivate habits of discipline that are good for you and honoring to God." And then Paul gets very specific:

> For this is the will of God, your sanctification;
> that is, that you abstain from sexual immorality
> (1 Thess. 4:3).

Understand, most of the ancient Thessalonian Christians were new in the faith, some of them not more than a week or two old in the Lord. They were fresh out of a sex-saturated society. Furthermore, there was never an age in all of history where marriage was taken so lightly and when divorce was so easy. In ancient Greece, these things were at their all-time low.

> Long ago Demosthenes had written: "We keep prostitutes for pleasure; we keep mistresses for the day to day needs of the body; we keep wives for the begetting of children and for the faithful guardianship of our homes. So long as a man supported his wife and family there was no shame whatsoever in extra-marital affairs."[15]

And yet, in spite of their culture, Paul says to them, *"In your morals, obey God by abstaining."* He begins: "This is the will of God." You don't even have to pray about it, asking God how He would have you live regarding sexual purity. It is clear: ". . . abstain from sexual immorality." *Apekomai* is the word translated "abstain." It means "to go away from, to depart, to be distant, to keep hands off." I call that emphatic. The word "abstain" is rarely used in Scripture, but when it is, it means just that. In one place, "abstain from meats." In another place, "abstain from fleshly lusts." In yet another place, "abstain from every form of evil." Each time, *apekomai*.

In the Christian faith, unlike the pagan faith, Paul taught them that sexual purity is significant. It is tied in directly with pleasing and obeying God. Morality and the worship of the living God go together. How? The answer is a total abstaining from sexual immorality. Hands off, no contact! How broad is this word for sexual immorality? It is the Greek term *porneia* ("pornography"), which includes homosexuality, incestuous relationships, unnatural acts with beasts and animals, premarital sexual relationships, and extramarital sex. It covers it all.

The answer to one's inability to refrain from lust, of course, is marriage. And if not marriage, then what? Abstain, plain and simple. If single, hands off! If divorced and not remarried? Hands off! Stay out of bed with anybody else, same or opposite sex . . . abstain. Among many other benefits, it is the safest route to take.

Several years ago I saw a cartoon that communicated this fact rather clearly. A grandson asks his grandfather, "Gee, Granddad, your generation didn't have all these social diseases. What did you wear to have safe sex?" Unhesitatingly, the old fellow responded, "A wedding ring."

This fourth verse of 1 Thessalonians 4 includes the statement that: "Each of you know how to possess his own vessel." New Testament authorities disagree whether "vessel" refers to one's wife or to one's body. Perhaps for the sake of illustration, we will use "body." It's this idea: That each of you know how to maintain control over your own body in sanctification and honor.

I love the way Paul emphasizes "know *how* to do it." He's being practical.

Verse 5 talks about being in control of our body when we are alone, and verse 6 addresses being in control when we are with others.

When alone . . . not in lustful passion, like the Gentiles who do not know God (v. 5).

When it has to do with anything that stimulates the path toward *porneia,* I repeat, abstain! May I get specific? It would include X-rated films and pornographic literature that prompt lurid mental pictures, stimulating sexual desires. Abstain! Conversations and discussions that arouse the same . . . parties and pastimes, along with sensual activities that seduce us and weaken our resistance. Abstain! Certain friends who are bad for us and weaken our moral standards . . . drugs . . . alcohol . . . sexually stimulating music . . . *anything* that externally adds to the breakdown of your moral fiber. Abstain!

If you cannot handle the movies on cable television, get rid of it! If you are in a hotel room where sexually explicit films are available, don't turn it on! "Don't be a fool; leave it off!" It's a matter of saying a loud "No!" to yourself.

When with others . . . And that no man transgress and defraud his brother in the matter because the Lord is the avenger in all these things, just as we also told you before and solemnly warned you.

This has reference to deceiving others or drawing them into the practice that we are engaged in, or for that matter, falling into seductive traps. Biting the bait. It would include any kind of indecent practices carried on secretly and promiscuously . . . with another man's wife or another woman's husband. I must also add, with one's own child or stepchild. With one's stepmother or stepfather. In the blended families of our day, incest is an increasing problem. And if you are engaged in it, you need to know it is not only an illicit, indecent practice, it is a criminal act, which should be reported. Whatever it takes, it is to be stopped! And if you are a mother tolerating it with a daughter or a stepdaughter, such passivity cannot continue. These things are not to be tolerated.

Verse 7 puts the capstone on all this:

For God has not called us for the purpose of impurity, but in sanctification.

In other words, God has called us to be people of moral purity. Why? Because He has our good at heart. This high standard of sexual conduct is not judgment, it is needed assistance. This is great coaching—counsel on how to stay free of disease and emotionally healthy. Furthermore, whoever heeds these warnings will not have to face the decision of whether or not to get an abortion. "Stay morally pure" is the best advice you could give your child, your teenager, the young adult who still lives in your home, yes, even yourself. This is straight talk from the Book.

The lingering warning is clear: *In obedience to God's command against immorality . . . RESIST!*

Before moving on to the next significant scripture, let me share with you how seriously I apply these warnings. I counsel pastors of churches not to go out to lunch with their secretaries alone. Don't sit alone with them in a car. Take your wife along. I counsel businessmen to do the same. Don't travel with your other-sex partner in the business. Bring someone else along. Refrain even from the appearance of evil. Play it smart! Don't give the devil an opportunity. One more time: *abstain!* The good news is this: Because you've played it smart, you've played it safe, and you've walked in obedience, chances are good you won't get in a jam where lust takes charge.

First Corinthians 6. This is a different scripture, but we're still in the same era. It's the same writer, another city. But don't think because we've left Thessalonica that we've come to "prudish Corinth." On the contrary! You know what the other word for fornication was in the days of Paul? *Corinthianize.* If you had a wild night . . . if you engaged in some kind of sexual orgy, or went to a drinking bash with a bunch of your buddies . . . you Corinthianized. Those ancient Greeks were the early playboys who gave themselves to lust, even in the worship of their pagan gods. There were priestesses who stayed at the temple strictly for the sexual pleasures of men. As we've already seen, this was no puritanical society back in the first century.

Between 1 Corinthians 6:15 and 20, the same word is used six times. Read the following very carefully:

> Do you not know that your *bodies* are members of Christ? Shall I then take away the members of Christ and make them members of a harlot? May it never be! Or do you not know that the one who joins himself to a harlot is one *body* with her? For He says, "THE TWO WILL BECOME ONE FLESH." But the one who joins himself to the Lord is one spirit with Him. Flee immorality. Every other sin that a man commits is outside the *body*, but the immoral man sins against his own *body*. Or do you not know that your *body* is a temple of the Holy Spirit who is in you, whom you have from God, and that you are not your own? For you have been bought with a price; therefore glorify God in your *body* [emphasis mine].

The apostle's concern here is directly related to one's physical body. The general context is the inappropriate connection of the body to that which is specifically described as *porneia*, the same term we found in the previous scripture.

Let me put it this way. When someone comes to know the Lord Jesus Christ as Savior, there is a bonding that takes place, like the meshing of gears with one another, like glue between two blocks of wood. You are linked together in a bond. Such linking results in becoming members of one another. A major problem occurs, however, when there is sexual involvement outside the bonds of monogamy. What occurs is a fracture in that spiritual bonding. Because the divine mystical union is violated, the bond is broken. As you become a member with another sexual partner, outside marriage, you break this mystical bond between you and the Lord. Such promiscuity takes a *devastating* toll on your life. It opens the door to all kinds of other violations. And sometimes this leaves you irreparably damaged and scarred.

I think this is what Paul has in mind when he writes with such passion at the end of chapter 9 of this same letter:

But I buffet my body [it's the word for beating oneself black and blue] and make it my slave, lest possibly, after I have preached to others, I myself should be disqualified [*adokimos* . . . disapproved].

It seems as if he's saying, "Due to the fracturing of that mystical bond, due to that violation, I forfeit the right to minister as I once ministered."

This has led me to adopt what some have called an extreme position, but I think it makes sense. When there is repeated sexual failure among ministers, they should relinquish the responsibility of high profile public leadership. Once there is recovery following full repentance, they can minister in various capacities. I find nothing wrong with that. But I have strong reservations with an individual who has fallen repeatedly still being granted a platform to preach as he once preached. I think one in that category forfeits such rights. There has been too great a violation, a break of the mystical bond. There are tragic consequences that follow this failure, and this is one of them.

Now we can understand why the statement found in 1 Corinthians 6:18 is so terribly important:

> Flee immorality. Every other sin that a man commits is outside the body, but the immoral man sins against his own body.

In this case, and only in this case, "the body is the instrument of sin and becomes the subject of the damage wrought," says A. T. Robertson.[16]

In gluttony, food is taken into the body but the sin of gluttony is from without, outside the body. In armed robbery, a crime committed against another, the body, of course, holds the weapon, But the body isn't the instrument of the sin. Only in sexual immorality is it actually and literally the instrument of sin, and thereby creates a *damage* in the psyche, the soulish, mystical part of one's being. Sexual sins are considered unique by the Lord.

There is further application here. We are seeing in our day a growing threat with AIDS directly linked (in most cases) to homosexual and extramarital sexual relations. God's Word says it boldly: "Flee immorality!" The lingering warning is clear: *For the sake of bodily health and remaining bonded to Christ, RUN!* Strong words, I realize, but not impossible. You can do it. God can give you that kind of power and grace. Not only would it enable us to take a giant step to curbing the AIDS dilemma, certainly the ever-increasing number of abortions would be greatly reduced.

Second Corinthians 12. Again we are reading the words of the same era, actually only a few months later. And they are written to the same people in the same church, on the same subject. Paul is thinking about returning to Corinth for a visit but he admits that he is afraid. In fact, the last two verses of 2 Corinthians 12 begin, "I am afraid . . . I am afraid."

> For I am afraid that perhaps when I come I may find you to be not what I wish and may be found by you to be not what you wish; that perhaps there may be strife, jealousy, angry tempers, disputes, slanders, gossip, arrogance, disturbances.

He is saying in effect: "I'm afraid of finding the same schism that's been there much too long, and I want you to get it cleaned up."

But he digs deeper in verse 21:

> I am afraid that when I come again my God may humiliate me before you, and I may mourn over many of those who have sinned in the past and not

repented of the impurity, immorality and sensuality which they have practiced.

Because I am a pastor, I want to be a man of the Word. I would wish the same for you. I want the Bible to guide us. I don't want to give you just good human counsel with helpful psychological techniques or merely practical ways to solve your moral struggles. I want you to see *from Scripture* what God has said about that problem and how you can handle it. Again and again I have found that there is nothing like God's Word to solve long-standing struggles and to bring cleansing and healing.

Three words are used in verse 21—three distinct words that describe disgraceful practices. The first one is translated "impurity," *akatharsia.* We get the word "cathartic" from it. It is a generic term for "uncleanness." *Akatharsia* would include covetousness, greed, wrong motives, even idolatry and sex sins. He writes, "I am afraid that when I come I will find some of you still engaged in an unrepented lifestyle of *akatharsia.* "

There's a second factor that concerns him, so he adds, "I'm afraid I'll find *porneia* still there as well." He wrote of it earlier (we examined it in 1 Corinthians 6). "I'm afraid when I come I will discover that there are sexual acts going on that are impure and weakening to monogamous relationships, and I will be humiliated. I will be ashamed."

Third, he states, "I may find sensuality." This third term is the tough one. *Aselgeia* is an unusual

Greek term. Problem is there is no translatable English equivalent for it. In general, it means "a wanton defiance of public decency." One scholar declares:

> There was *uncleanness (aselgeia)*. Here is an untranslatable word. It does not only mean sexual uncleanness. It is sheer wanton insolence. As Basil defined it, "It is that attitude of the soul which has never borne and never will bear the pain of discipline." It is the wanton insolence that knows no restraint, that has no sense of the decencies of things, that will dare anything that wanton caprice demands, which is careless of public opinion and its own good name so long as it gets what it wants. Josephus ascribes it to Jezebel who built a temple to Baal in the very city of God itself. The basic Greek sin was *hubris*, and *hubris* is that proud insolence which gives neither God nor man his place. *Aselgeia* is the insolently selfish spirit, which is lost to honour and lost to shame, and which will take what it wants where it wants it in shameless disregard of God and man.[17]

Clearly, the apostle is concerned about sexual addiction . . . an addiction to sexual indecency.

Do you detect the downward trend? *Akatharsia* comes first, which leads to *porneia*, and finally *aselgeia*—a wanton defiance of public shame, leaving one without a feeling of embarrassment.

The lingering warning? *To be free from the bondage of sexual misconduct, REPENT!* As we saw so clearly in chapter 2, I'm talking about more than confession. Repentance is beyond confession. Remember? To confess is to admit, to agree with God that something is wrong and displeases Him, claiming His forgiveness. Repentance is more. It is a deliberate turning away from wrong, changing one's mind, removing all traces, relinquishing all connections, so that the bond is no longer broken and Christ reigns supreme, without a rival.

How far do I believe one should go to break sexual addiction? I'd suggest the burning of all pornographic literature. Not just discarding it, but burning it. And what about friendships that pull you into questionable areas? Get rid of those so-called friendships! Actually, they are not friendships; they are destructive and disruptive relationships. And if you are living with someone outside of wedlock, *move out!* It will result in terrible consequences. Perhaps the worst of all is the continuation of sexual addiction for you and your partner. There is a downward cycle of sensuality that doesn't get better; it always degenerates. By and by it will destroy your life. And if you don't? Rest assured, "God is the avenger." Again I say these are strong words, but like radical surgery, they will make it possible for you to survive.

Several Helpful Solutions with Personal Benefits

There are times in my life when it helps to spell things out in an oversimplified fashion. Somehow it enables me to get a handle on things. Perhaps this is one of those times. I realize we've covered an

enormous amount of serious ground. Responding
correctly is very important. So allow me to suggest
several helpful ideas that have worked for others. I
hope they will work for you as well. Here's an A-B-
C-D plan of correction:

A. *Acknowledge.* Hold nothing back as you acknowledge the impurity. The benefit of a full-on
acknowledgment is that it will heal the distance
between you and your Lord. Acknowledge the
bondage. Acknowledge the involvement. Say it to
your God. Then say it to somebody who can help
you, not just to yourself. Acknowledge it to someone
you respect. No struggle just quietly dissolves. The
first step to victory is an admission of the battle.

B. *Break.* I mean by this, break all connections.
The benefit of this is that it stops the cycle. Unless
connections are broken, the addiction won't cease.
The flesh dies hard. Get rid of the stacks of *Playboy.*
Stay away from the pornography. If you have long-
standing connections at distant places where you
travel, break those ties. Toss out the little black
book. Unless you make a break like this, the battle
will continue to rage and you will become another
casualty.

C. *Communicate.* Express your need for others'
strength. The benefit is it will make you accountable.
If you've never been accountable before, I suggest
you make every effort to become part of a small
group of people (of the same sex) where you can talk
openly about the battle and the difficulties you live
with. Perhaps your church offers adult fellowships

or accountability groups. They are the lifeline to recovery and full restoration.

D. *Determine.* Determine to abstain. You may have a past which is littered with incredible things that you would find embarrassing to admit even to a close friend. There is absolutely no reason to continue. Stop it today! The benefit is that it will free you to be all God meant you to be. Furthermore, it could save you from sure tragedy that could be just around the corner.

And in case you need a boost to get started . . . an unforgettable reminder that God means business, I close with a true story. The names are fictitious, but the story is true.

Clara and Chester's twenty-eight-year-old marriage was a good one. Not the most idyllic, but good. By now they had three grown children who loved them dearly. They were also blessed with sufficient financial security to allow them room to dream about a retirement home, so they began looking for one. A widower we'll call Sam was selling his place. They liked it a lot and they returned home to talk and to make their plans. Months passed.

Last fall Clara told Chester she wanted a divorce. He went numb. After all these years, why? How could she deceive him? How could she have been nursing such a scheme while they were looking at a retirement home? She said she hadn't been . . . not for that long. Actually, this was a rather recent decision now that she had found another man. Who? Clara admitted it was Sam, the owner of the house they were considering. She had inadvertently run into him several weeks after they had discussed the sale. They had a cup of coffee together; later the next week they went out to dinner. For several weeks they had been seeing each other privately and were now sexually involved. Since they were "in love," there was no turning back. Not even the kids, who hated the idea, could dissuade their mother.

On the day Clara was to leave, Chester walked through the kitchen toward the garage. Realizing Clara would be gone when he returned, he hesitated, "Well, hon, I guess this is the last time . . ." and his voice dissolved as he broke into sobs. She felt awkward, so she hurriedly got her things together, backed out of the driveway, and never looked back. She drove north to meet Sam. Less than two weeks after she moved in with her new lover, Sam was seized with a heart attack and lingered a few hours. The following morning Sam died.

When it comes to morality, God is serious . . . as serious as a heart attack.

A Time for
Strong Resolve

I began this book by mentioning that I am a pastor.
To some, that suggests a world that is sheltered, free
from life's ugly side, and protected by the walls of
a church. Whoever thinks that doesn't understand
either the ministry in general or this minister in
particular.

I know of few professions more in touch—and I
mean closely in touch—with the raw realities of life.
I could fill a book much larger than this with one

story after another of broken lives, fractured marriages, heartaches, terminal illnesses, calamities, confrontations, disappointments, demonic attacks, murders, abuse, assaults, addictions, and of course abortions. So it is with most who serve in ministry, I can assure you.

Early in 1990 Cynthia and I had the privilege of ministering to a large number of fellow ministers and their mates. While rubbing shoulders with them, we heard firsthand one incredible story after another, most of them related to the categories I have mentioned above. What a week! If we had ever been tempted to think we were alone in the things we were personally encountering, that idea was quickly shattered. Exhausted, we sat down on the plane to fly home following those eight days and I was suddenly overcome with tears. Though I'm not one who weeps easily, I felt overwhelmed with emotion and weighed down by the times in which we are living. I gave God thanks for my brothers and sisters in ministry who serve so faithfully amidst incredible pressures and against insuperable odds. I couldn't stop the tears for a couple of minutes, a most unusual reaction on my part. To be honest with you, I'm not completely over those feelings, though I have had time to get some perspective as time has passed.

On our way home I took out a pad of paper and began to record several thoughts that grew out of those days we had been together. I had no idea back then that they would ever find their way into a book, but here they are. Actually, these were the very thoughts that stimulated me to address some of the things I've been writing about in these chapters.

Four Observations about Our Times

First, *the enemy is hard at work.* We may have turned the most significant corner of the twentieth century as we step into its final decade. In light of the things I am confronting and my colleagues in ministry are dealing with, this is no time to slacken our efforts. The enemy may have always been hard at it in the "secular cosmos," but I am more aware than ever that he has now made a frontal assault on the church at large. There is every reason to believe that he is alive and well in our midst!

He and his demons are directly involved in assaulting and assassinating the lives of men who were once strong in the pulpit. He is cutting the feet out from under once-respected and high-profile Christian individuals who were effective and full of zeal, courageous in songs and sermons. He isn't letting up, either. Religious leaders, counselors, media personalities, and educators are falling like ducks full of buckshot. If he has done anything in this final decade, he has rolled up his sleeves and intensified his efforts, especially against minister-types, hoping to discredit even those who have integrity. Whoever is not aware of overt enemy attacks in these days qualifies as a human ostrich.

Second, *the pressure and the needs are enormous on people of all walks of life.* Have you begun to notice that? More and more of those who are engaged in some kind of leadership are finding themselves oppressed and depressed. You may be in evangelistic leadership or you may be in teaching leadership or you may be a leader in a mission outreach or in educational leadership. Chances are good if you are a Christian and you are influencing people for the cause of Christ, you are under pressure such as you've never known before. I cannot remember another time when so many feel so overwhelmed by pressure.

My Bible is open to a couple of verses of Scripture. First Peter 5:8–9 seems better able to say what I'm trying to express.

> Be of sober spirit, be on the alert. Your adversary, the devil, prowls about like a roaring lion, seeking someone to devour (v. 8).

Let me ask why are we to be on the alert? Why does he write that with such passion? The answer is clear: "your adversary." He isn't the adversary of some distant body of monks and missionaries, some small group of influential leaders who are doing top-secret work or strategic ministry. He is *"your* adversary," fellow Christian, fellow minister, fellow leader, fellow teacher, fellow elder, fellow broadcaster. He is *"your* adversary," Christian parents, Christian business man or woman. And who is this adversary of ours? He is identified as "the devil." And what is his method? He "prowls about." Now, that's pretty descriptive. There is no noise. He isn't marching to some heavy cadence. He is much more subtle and sneaky than that. Invisibly, insidiously, cleverly, brilliantly, with stealth and strategy, "your adversary prowls about like a roaring lion." Don't miss this: He is on a pursuit. And he is not hoping to munch on a midafternoon snack; he is deliberately "seeking someone to *devour.*" Do you want to take this personally? If so, insert your name in place of "someone." If it will help you; I'll do it too: "Like a roaring lion, he is seeking to devour Chuck Swindoll, or the Swindoll family, or the Swindoll ministry, or the integrity of the Swindoll name." Frightening thought! He is deliberately prowling about to ruin, to discredit, to cast a cloud over, to weaken the impact of our influence. So? So "be of sober spirit, be on the alert."

Now what are we to do with an enemy like that? Run and hide? Hardly. This is no day for religious wimps. Verse 9 commands us to do something. "Resist him" is the biblical imperative. And be certain your resistance is "firm in faith." Not in the energy of your own strength, but "firm in faith," remembering that you are not alone. The verse concludes:

> . . . knowing that the same experiences of suffering are being accomplished by your brethren who are in the world (v. 9).

Because of Cynthia's and my involvement early in 1990, I have a whole new group of brothers and sisters I didn't know as recently as the year before— people who are in the same world I am in, the same world you are in, and they are going through the same stuff you and I are going through. We are all in this together, for the long haul.

Third, *the temptation to overreact is great, perhaps greater than ever.* By overreacting I mean, on the one hand, to cave in. The pressure mounts, greater and greater tests come, needs increase, and it is easy just to succumb, quietly surrender, and compromise the message. Soften the response and don't make waves. Just keep the peace at any price.

On the other hand, an overreaction would be to yield to the temptation to fight back, to scream, to burn the candle at both ends, and intensify all efforts to the breaking point. If you are being shouted at, shout back! If you are being accused, accuse in return! If you are being assaulted, then roll up your sleeves and find a way to return the assault.

The ultimate overreaction, of course, is to quit, just fold up the book and go into some other work, just get away from the pressure. It is a little disturbing for me to realize how many in ministry today, live in confusion or feel whipped like stray dogs or intimidated by a few powerful people in their church. Equally disturbing is the realization of how many there are in ministry who are angry or have become disillusioned and bitter. If God ever wanted to do a significant work, it is *now* —right now in the final era of this century. For some of us, it could be our last full decade. Actually, we have no promise of seeing the end of this century. All of us by grace have been allowed to witness the beginning of it.

But the end of it? Maybe not. These may very well be our last few years. How important not to end them with a whimper.

Fourth, *this is a time for strong resolve.* We cannot, we dare not just sit back and calmly hope for the best. Those with small children cannot simply fold their hands and blandly shrug their shoulders and slip quietly into the workplace. The answer is not just earning more money to give them the best, hoping they turn out right. They need attention and training, your time and discipline—and love. They need you. They need solid, confident, authentic models. They need your touch, your affirmation. Parents, this is a time for strong resolve.

It is also a time of strong resolve for people in education and counseling as well as in pulpits, for those who write music, as well as those who write books. For those in business as well as those in professions. These days require a strong resolve. We really don't have forever, fellow pilgrim.

Billy Graham's excellent book, released far back in the late sixties, entitled *World Aflame,* strikes a similar chord.

> In a declining culture, one of its characteristics is that the ordinary people are unaware of what is happening. Only those who know and can read the signs of decadence are posing the questions that as yet have no answers. Mr. Average Man is comfortable in his complacency and as unconcerned as a silverfish ensconced in a carton of discarded

magazines on world affairs. He is not asking any questions, because his social benefits from the government give him a false security. This is his trouble and his tragedy. Modern man has become a spectator of world events, observing on his television screen without becoming involved. He watches the ominous events of our times pass before his eyes, while he sips his beer in a comfortable chair. He does not seem to realize what is happening to him. He does not understand that his world is on fire and that he is about to be burned with it.[18]

A Call for Balance

Now understand, as I conclude this book with a number of resolutions, that I am not advocating an out-of-balanced zeal. We don't need iron-fisted leadership or an absence of vulnerability among those who are God's spokesmen and women. I am not suggesting that there be influence by intimidation or by mind control or by verbal threats. You who know me well know that I stand against everything those things represent. Though times are tough, I am not calling for bullies in pulpits or for unaccountable, unteachable, and inaccessible leaders in places of importance. First and foremost, I want to promote the idea of modeling servanthood, discipline, truth, and unguarded authenticity. Our goal must continue toward patterning our lives after the One who came before us and has gone on beyond us, Jesus Christ, God's Son. He came, remember, full of grace and truth, the perfect balance.

Nevertheless, we do need strong resolve. Without it, I am convinced that Christians cannot victoriously handle the next ten years, certainly as the troubling hints on the horizon begin to emerge into reality. Neither do I think it is God's will that we merely yawn our way through the maze of this pressurized decade, taking our cues from the media. What strength of character we must have to make a difference in the 1990s!

While in prayer about so much of this, I was led ever so gently back into the great Book of Psalms. How unusual it seemed to me that God would lead me there. Like you, I have always thought of the Psalms as a book of magnificent praise and quiet devotion. But the more I pored over Psalm 102, the more it seemed to pulsate with exclamation points that were inherent in the biblical text.

Before concluding this book with five strong resolves for the decade, let me set the stage by sharing some observations from this and a couple other psalms. We are told that this particular song is "a prayer of the afflicted, when he is faint, and pours out his complaint before the Lord." We don't know who "he" is, not exactly. We know who wrote Psalm 101, because the superscription declares, "A Psalm of David." And the same for Psalm 103, "A Psalm of David." But there is no man, by name, connected with Psalm 102. Whoever he was, he was "afflicted." Maybe he was one of the lonely prophets, perhaps a priest. He could have been a troubled father who is never named in Scripture, but for some reason the

Spirit of God chose his song and included the stanzas of it in the sacred text. It is a moving account of a man in need. He is pleading:

> Hear my prayer, O Lord! And let my cry for help come to Thee (v. 1).

I can just see his hands lifted in a dark place. He pleads to be heard, to be rescued and given divine assistance. He then writes with urgency and vivid imagery:

> Do not hide Thy face from me in the day of my distress; incline Thine ear to me; in the day when I call answer me quickly. For my days have been consumed in smoke, and my bones have been scorched like a hearth. My heart has been smitten like grass and has withered away . . . (vv. 2–3).

Do you feel the emotion of the psalm? "My days, my bones, my heart, are consumed, scorched, smitten, like grass, and withered away." He is troubled over his *loss of motivation and passion*. He struggles because, by his own admission, "something is withering inside me." His lack of zeal is wearing on him.

Those in ministry understand. The person who speaks for God knows the Lord's mandate. In spite of this, he can't get excited. There is nothing quite so depressing as feeling that the power has gone out of one's voice, or the passion that was once there is now missing . . . that there is indifference and apathy in place of motivation and direction. There are few sights more tragic than a leader who has lost the zest to lead. Maybe the psalmist was in that category.

Along with a loss of motivation and passion, he also confessed to a *loss of appetite*:

> Indeed, I forget to eat my bread. Because of the loudness of my groaning my bones cling to my flesh (v. 4–5).

Have you ever been so distressed, so discouraged, that fixing a meal seems a Herculean task? Or have you ever felt so low, the thought of stopping and eating seems a futile interruption to your grief and mourning? Involuntarily you lose weight. At such low times you think, *When will I ever get back on my feet?*

There is also a *loss of self-respect.* Look at how the psalmist refers to himself:

> I resemble a pelican of the wilderness; I have become like an owl of the waste places. I lie awake, I have become like a lonely bird on a housetop (vv. 6–7).

The man is near bottom. He reminds me of some I've met who were once strong and confident in ministry, but no longer. Surprisingly, many in ministry are like that. I don't know when my heart has been so moved over those who have God's message and have the gifts, the calling and the place of authority to declare it . . . but they are not doing it because of distress.

Look at verse 11:

> My days are like a lengthened shadow; and I wither away like grass.

Instead of feeling full of hope and direction, he suffers a severe *loss of determination*. He is being eaten alive by anxiety. He is no match for the days he faces.

Psalm 109 is a similar-sounding psalm. David begins with a passionate request:

> O God of my praise, do not be silent! (v. 1).

Have you ever begun a prayer like that? "Lord, listen up! Please, Lord, listen! Don't turn Your back on me. Don't ignore me, Lord." That is the plea of verse 1. "O God of my praise, don't be silent!" The implication is, "Speak, enter into my world." And here he realizes the causes of his discouragement. "They" [the ubiquitous "they"]. They are always there . . . always those people, those sources of pressure and anxiety. We all encounter them.

> For they have opened the wicked and deceitful mouth against me; they have spoken against me with a lying tongue (v. 2).

Remember his command, "Don't be silent, Lord. Listen to where I am."

They have also surrounded me with words of hatred, and fought against me without cause. In return for my love they act as my accusers; but I am in prayer. Thus they have repaid me evil for good, and hatred for my love (vv. 3–5).

"Lord, don't be silent. I'm withering under the accusations and the evil, hateful attacks. Speak, Lord. Enter in. Act. Defend!" Like so many in our day, the man can't seem to get up for the challenge of his times. To him, the Lord seems like a distant Deity.

Quickly, one more psalm of a similar nature— Psalm 120. Again, there's no author named, but it is yet another plea. The writer is in trouble and admits it. (One of the wonderful things about prayer is you can tell it all, and God won't tell anybody. You can unload your heart and He will hear, accept, understand, and renew.) Read the psalm slowly, with feeling:

In my trouble I cried to the Lord, and He answered me. Deliver my soul, O Lord, from lying lips, from a deceitful tongue. What shall be given to you, and what more shall be done to you, you deceitful tongue? Sharp arrows of the warrior, with the burning coals of the broom tree. Woe is me, for I sojourn in Meshech, for I dwell among the tents of Kedar! Too long has my soul had its dwelling with those who hate peace. I am for peace, but when I speak, they are for war (Psalm 120:1–7).

He has quite a dilemma! He speaks for peace, but he is surrounded by those who want to hate and want to fight back. He prefers to press on, but they want to hold back and complain.

I don't know what all of this is saying to you, but none can deny the scenery is stormy and the battle is raging. It reminds me so much of our times; ours is a time for keen resolve, but the edge is blunted by so many obstacles. As I wrote earlier, we can't just drift aimlessly through the nineties and expect to do much that will make a difference. These are tough times. The enemy is at work. Pressure is mounting. I am convinced we need to be people of strong resolve if we hope to cope with and shape our world.

This idea of resolutions is not original or new. Jonathan Edwards, who lived between 1703 and 1758, was a brilliant philosopher-theologian, and a powerful preacher of grace. Listen to a few of his resolutions.

- Resolved, That I will do whatsoever I think to be most to the glory of God, and my own good, profit, and pleasure, in the whole of my duration; without any consideration of the time, whether now, or never so many myriads of ages hence.

- Resolved, to do whatever I think to be my duty, and most for the good and advantage of mankind in general.

- Resolved, never to lose one moment of time, but to improve it in the most profitable way I possibly can.

- Resolved, to live with all my might, while I do live.

- Resolved, Never to do any thing, which I should be afraid to do if it were the last hour of my life.

- Resolved, Never to speak evil of any one, so that it shall tend to his dishonour, more or less, upon no account except for some real good.

- Resolved, To study the Scriptures so steadily, constantly, and frequently, as that I may find, and plainly perceive, myself to grow in the knowledge of the same.[19]

Such resolutions help shake us free from the discouragement of our times. They give our "withering grass" new life. They help make us into people of character rather than guardians of our reputation as we conclude this century.

John Wooden, former coach of the UCLA Bruins basketball team, including ten national championship years, writes:

Be more concerned with your character than with your reputation. Your character is what you really are while your reputation is merely what others think you are.[20]

Strong Resolve for Tough Times

Borrowing from Wooden's words, I urge you to care more about your character than your reputation as you invest your energies in the nineties. I think strong resolutions will help make that happen. If you and I hope to live above the moral drag of the decade, we will need to counteract strength with strength. Furthermore, if we plan to penetrate our times and be a positive influence for righteousness in a world that is rapidly losing its way, we cannot afford to wander through these years without a compass of commitment.

I promise to make these my resolutions for the new decade. I challenge you to do the same.

RESOLVED—*to be alert to the presence of evil and the strategy of the adversary.* Admittedly, I know some of what we face does not come directly from the devil. But I am confident that much of it does, if not directly at least indirectly. Our adversary wants nothing more than to demoralize, discourage, and discredit every one of us. He is the original murderer, the first deceiver. As we saw earlier, he is subtle. He is invisible. He masks and masquerades. He has insidious plans. His strategies are clever, smarter than you and I would ever imagine. We cannot afford the luxury of ignorance. We must know our enemy and be alert to his presence and to the ugly workings of evil in the 1990s. *I so resolve.*

RESOLVED—*to stay fervent in prayer.* I want to be more a minister of prayer in the 1990s than I have ever been through any other decade of ministry. I resolve, and if you are with me, you, too, resolve to stay fervent in prayer, not hesitating to call down supernatural assistance or, when necessary, divine discipline.

All the way through the psalms I read courageous words, strong words. The psalmist pleads with his Lord in prayer, and challenges God to confuse the enemy, to silence the chronic complainer and critic, to remove the cause of unrest, to make miserable the one who makes war. Those are strong prayers.

Let's make the 1990s a decade of passionate petition and courageous intercession. Let's fight our best battles on our knees. Rather than becoming better at debate and more clever in our sarcasm, let's quickly drop to our knees and do our best work there. And if it's some great cause you are pursuing, if it's some great vision you are entertaining, if it's some great concern you are wrestling with, whether it be worldwide or in your own tiny cubicle of life, take it first to God—to stay fervent in prayer through the decade. *I so resolve.*

RESOLVED—*to refuse to retaliate in the energy of the flesh.* Revenge is a dead-end street. But it comes so naturally! When we are swung at, the great tendency is to swing back. Most of us were taught how to do that. What a time-wasting effort, since it leads only to more skirmishes. Furthermore, there is no stopping point. And worst of all, the adversary of our souls *loves* it when we take him on in our own flesh. Every time we make that mistake, we lose.

Several years ago a radio listener called me. He was a new Christian, full of vim and vigor . . . lots of zeal but little knowledge. He blurted out, "I just wanna tell you, Chuck, I'm a new Christian . . . and I'm ready to take on the devil one-on-one!" *O, boy,* I thought. So I said, "Wait. Wait. Don't kid yourself." He didn't quite understand. He wondered about my reluctance. Interestingly, he called me again just the other day. Rather sheepishly, he asked: "Chuck, remember me? I'm the one who called you and said . . . ." I remembered his voice and said, "I remember." He quickly responded, "I just want you to know I'm not ready any longer to take on the devil one-on-one." I said, "You've learned?" He said, "Man, have I!" The "arm of flesh" won't cut it when it comes to being overmatched.

That is like my taking on Larry Bird or Michael Jordan one-on-one in a game of hoops. In order for me to take on either one of them, I need a substitute. I need Magic Johnson! One-on-one he could handle those guys . . . but I wouldn't stand a chance. If I'm lucky, I would get two dribbles, then watch either one of them do a lay-up. I can't *do it,* because they are better, stronger, taller, more capable, more gifted. And so is your adversary! If you attempt to retaliate in the energy of the flesh, you will experience defeat again and again. Refuse to retaliate!

Joseph wouldn't do it with his brothers. David wouldn't do it with Saul. Paul wouldn't do it with Alexander the coppersmith. His last lines in the dungeon were, "Lord, You take care of Alexander the coppersmith." This does not mean that you won't ever confront. And it doesn't mean that as a leader you don't have to make tough decisions or deal with wrong. But it means you are not, by nature, a fighter. And you will refuse to operate as a lone ranger.

Listen to The Living Bible's rendering of Psalm 5:8–10:

Lord, lead me as you promised me you would; otherwise my enemies will conquer me. Tell me clearly what to do, which way to turn. For they cannot speak one truthful word. Their hearts are filled to the brim with wickedness. Their suggestions are full of the stench of sin and death. Their tongues are filled with flatteries to gain their wicked ends. O God, hold them responsible. Catch them in their own traps; let them fall beneath the weight of their own transgressions, for they rebel against you.

What wise perspective. The enemies of righteousness are not your enemies, they are enemies of God. He can handle them. Let Him. Tell Him. Release them to Him. Whenever we retaliate in the flesh the devil is given an advantage. At those times, he comes in like a flood. In these pressurized days, we must refuse to retaliate in the energy of the flesh. *I so resolve.*

RESOLVED—*to refuse to slacken, surrender, or quit the path of obedience no matter how intense the pressure.*

Ours has become a soft, just-back-off-and-quit generation. In many ways the 1980s represented a decade of greed, a generation of self-satisfaction. Somehow, that twisted emphasis has led to a strange conclusion. We are now more prone to give up or take a path of least resistance when we face challenges. Many of us, raised by work-ethic parents, picked up that mentality, but some of our kids have not. And the whole idea of standing tall at tough times and standing like a steer in a blizzard at barren times or standing alone at tempting times is foreign to many of our younger adults. Chances are good your children are weaker than you are.

This is a time to embrace a strong resolve and to encourage all in our family to do the same. Let's stop the thinking that says if it's uncomfortable, then don't pursue; if it might offend someone, then don't make waves. Let's call to mind that obedience is a lonely path so we need to walk it together. I hope as you watch my life or as you hear my words or as you read what I write in the coming decade, you can say, there is a man who has not slackened or surrendered or quit the path of obedience. *I so resolve.*

Finally, RESOLVED—*to seek to glorify the Lord God and to trust the Word of God, regardless.* Read those words once again, please. The key is *regardless.* How much do I mean that? I mean that more than pleasing people. I mean that more than promoting self. I mean that more than escaping affliction. The glory of God ultimately becomes the major filter of one's life. Whatever we do in word or deed, we are to do all in the name of the Lord Jesus, for the glory of God the Father, in the power of the Holy Spirit. What a way to live! This need not mean we become killjoys, grim reapers in a day of joy. No. No one has a freer conscience than one whose conscience has been cleansed and whose heart has been washed by the blood. No one has a reason to laugh at life like the believer in Christ.

It is now essential that we have this dual objective if we hope to represent the cause of Christ in the decade of the 1990s: to seek to glorify the Lord God and to trust the Word of God, regardless. *I so resolve.*

For the sake of emphasis, let me list these five resolutions:

- Resolved first—to be alert to the presence of evil and the strategy of the adversary.

- Resolved second—to stay fervent in prayer.

- Resolved third—to refuse to retaliate in the energy of the flesh.

- Resolved fourth—to refuse to slacken, surrender, or quit the path of obedience no matter how intense the pressure.

- Resolved fifth—to seek to glorify the Lord God and to trust the Word of God, regardless.

A Personal Word

My hope and prayer is that you will join me in this personal crusade for character. I promise to give myself to these truths, no matter what the future holds. Will you do the same?

It was in a strong sermon preached in 1531 that Martin Luther said some of the same things I have been emphasizing in this book. Though well over 450 years old, these words give me fresh courage and determination to stand firm in a day of eroding values.

Christendom must have people who can beat down their adversaries and opponents and tear off the devil's equipment and armor, that he may be brought into disgrace. But for this work, powerful warriors are needed, who are thoroughly familiar with the Scriptures and can contradict all false interpretations and take the sword from false teachers—that is, those very verses which false teachers use and turn them round upon them so that they fall back defeated. But as not all Christians can be so capable in defending the Word and articles of their creed, they must have teachers and preachers who study the Scriptures and have daily fellowship with it, so that they can fight for all the others. Yet each Christian should be so armed that he himself is sure of his belief and of the doctrine and is so equipped with the sayings from the Word of God that he can stand up against the devil and defend himself, when men seek to lead him astray.[21]

No question Luther was a man of enormous inner strength. Are you sure you have the power within to stand as he once stood? Throughout this book I have thrown down repeated challenges. From sanctity to morality, on issues ranging from abortion to abstinence, I have called for doing what is right, what is best, what pleases God rather than what pleases you or someone else. It takes supernatural power, I realize.

It is possible that you may not know the source of that power or how to tap into it personally. Such power comes from the Person of Jesus Christ, who died that you might live. He also arose from the dead and lives to give hope and strength to all who believe. He alone is able to provide the power and He is willing to do so for all who turn their lives over to Him. I would urge you to do that today, this very moment. As you turn to Him and trust Him with your whole heart, He will accept you into His family. The power you need will be yours to claim.

Without His presence in your life, there is no way you can expect to break the habits that control you or, for that matter, change the direction of your life. By taking care of first things first, however, you will be amazed at the hope and strength He will give, enabling you to become the kind of person you have wanted to be all your life—a person of inner strength, deep character, and strong resolve.

Endnotes

1. Dr. and Mrs. John C. Willke, *Abortion—Questions and Answers* (Cincinnati, OH: Hayes Publishing Co., 1988). Used by permission.

2. Taken from *Abortion* (Dallas, TX: *Christian Medical & Dental Society Journal*, Summer 1976, Volume VII, Number 3. © 1976 by the Christian Medical Society).

3. E. Fuller Torrey, taken from *Abortion* (Dallas, TX: *Christian Medical & Dental Society Journal*, Summer 1976, Volume VII, Number 3. © 1976 by the Christian Medical Society).

4. Gina Kolata, "Fewer Doctors Performing Abortions" (*The Los Angeles Daily Journal*, January 16, 1990), p. 20.

5. Statistics from Alan Guttmacher Institute, division of Planned Parenthood, New York, New York. Cited in *Rescue Update*, June/July 1989. Southern California Operation Rescue.

6. Ibid.

7. "American War Casualties." Used by permission of Right to Life of Greater Cincinnati.

8. Edward R. Dalglish, *Psalm Fifty-One in the Light of Near Eastern Patternism* (Leiden: T. J. Brill, 1962), p. 121.

9. Bruce Waltke, "Abortion," *Christian Medical & Dental Society Journal* (Summer 1976, Volume VII, Number 3. © 1976 by the Christian Medical Society).

10. C. Everett Koop. Cited in *One Church's Answer to Abortion* by Bill Hybels (Chicago: Moody Press), © 1986 by The Moody Bible Institute of Chicago, p. 22–23.

11. Paul E. Rockwell, M.D., "Month 2" *When You Were Formed in Secret* by Gary Bergel. Copyright © 1980, 1982, 1983, 1984, 1985, 1986, 1988 Intercessors for America. All rights reserved. Used by permission.

12. Ron Lee Davis, *Mistreated* (Portland, OR: Multnomah Press, 1989), pp. 137–138.

13. Bill Hybels, *One Church's Answer to Abortion* (Chicago, IL: Moody Press, 1986). © 1986 by The Moody Bible Institute of Chicago. Used by permission. pp. 16, 17, 18.

14. Roberta Kells Dorr, *David and Bathsheba* (Wheaton: Tyndale House Publishers, Inc., 1982), p. 238.

15. William Barclay, *The Daily Study Bible: The Letters to Philippians, Colossians and Thessalonians* (Edinburgh: The Saint Andrew Press, 1959), p. 231.

16. A. T. Robertson, *Word Pictures in the New Testament, The Epistles of Paul,* Vol. IV (Nashville, TN: Broadman Press, 1931), p. 122.

17. William Barclay, *The Daily Study Bible: The Letters to the Corinthians* (Edinburgh: The Saint Andrew Press, 1954), p. 296.

18. Billy Graham, *World Aflame* (Garden City, NY: Doubleday & Company, Inc.). Copyright © 1965 by Billy Graham.

19. From *The Works of Jonathan Edwards,* Vol. 1, pp. xx–xxii. Used by permission of Banner of Truth Trust.

20. John Wooden, *Great Quotes from Great Leaders,* compiled by Peggy Anderson. Copyright © 1989, Great Quotations, Inc.

21. From a sermon preached by Martin Luther in 1531. Taken from *A Mighty Fortress Is Our God, Illustrations and Meditations from the Life of Martin Luther.* Compiled by Pastor Mark Anderson and Marjorie Young.